Schools in the Forest

Schools in the Forest

How Grassroots Education Brought Political Empowerment to the Brazilian Amazon

Denis Lynn Daly Heyck

Kumarian Press
An Imprint of Stylus Publishing

Schools in the Forest:
How Grassroots Education Brought Political Empowerment to the Brazilian Amazon
Published in 2010 in the United States of America by Kumarian Press,
22883 Quicksilver Drive, Sterling, VA 20166 USA.

Design by Pro Production Graphic Services
Copyedit by Bob Land
Proofread by Beth Richards
Index by Robert Swanson
The text of this book is set in 11/14 Adobe Garamond

Printed in the USA on acid-free paper by Thomson-Shore.

⊚ The paper used in this publication meets the minimum requirements of the American
National Standard for Information Sciences—Permanence of Paper for printed Library
Materials, ANSI Z39.48–1984

Library of Congress Cataloging-in-Publication Data

Heyck, Denis Lynn Daly.
Schools in the forest : how grassroots education brought political
    empowerment to the Brazilian Amazon / Denis Heyck.
        p.   cm.
    Includes bibliographical references and index.
    ISBN 978-1-56549-350-6 (pbk. : alk. paper) — ISBN 978-1-56549-351-3
        (cloth : alk. paper)
    1. Projeto Seringueiro. 2. Fundamental education—Brazil. 3. Fundamental
education—Amazon River Region. 4. Rubber tappers—Education—Brazil.
5. Rubber tappers—Education—Amazon River Region. 6. Rubber tappers—
Brazil—Political activity. 7. Rubber tappers—Amazon River Region—Political
activity. I. Title.
    LC5163.B7H39   2010
    370.11'109811—dc22

                                                    2010011070

To Bill, Mary and Ronizia

Contents

Acknowledgments ix

Preface xi

Part I History

1 Acre: Land, People and Struggle 3

2 Lantern in the Forest:
Origins, Influences and Early Years of Projeto Seringueiro 19

3 Disarray, Renewal and Absorption 39

Part II Voices

4 Points of Light 63
Introduction, 63
Ademir Pereira Rodrigues, 64
Dercy Teles de Carvalho, 71
Antonia Pereira Vieira, 78

5 Reformers 85
Introduction, 85
Arnóbio "Binho" Marques Júnior, 86
Djalcir "Pingo" Ferreira, 95

6 From Projeto Seringueiro to Rural and Indigenous Education 109
Introduction, 109
Ivanilde Lopes da Silva, 110
Francisca "Chiquinha" das Chagas Souza da Silva, 118
Manoel Estébio Cavalcante da Cunha, 128

Part III Conclusion

Conclusion   149

Bibliography   159
Glossary of Portuguese Terms   165
Acronyms   167
Index   169
About the Author   179

Acknowledgments

Any story of popular empowerment is bound to have many key actors, and *Schools in the Forest* is no exception. I am deeply indebted to all those whose stories appear in this volume. They generously gave of their time, speaking with candor and eloquence of their experiences during times of hardship and hope.

Heartfelt thanks to Mary Allegretti, who with Chico Mendes conceived of the project and founded the first Projeto Seringueiro school. Mary welcomed me into her home and archives, offered her friendship, and advanced the project in essential ways. I owe a tremendous debt of gratitude to Ronizia Gonçalves, a valued friend for many years, who opened doors and hearts and minds in ways that only a trusted native of Rio Branco could do. To Charles Vieira I am grateful for enlightening conversations on the social movement in Rio Branco, including those on the road to Xapuri. Like the founders of Projeto Seringueiro themselves, I am much indebted to Dom Moacyr Grechi, archbishop of Rondônia, who helped me understand the role of Chico Mendes and the origins of the social movement in Acre.

I wish to thank Júlia Feitosa, Cila Pereira dos Santos, Raimunda Evangelista, Salustiano Diogo de Lima, and Graciete Zaire, whose interviews did not make their way into the volume, but whose valuable contributions did. Irmã Ignez of Xapuri on various occasions provided lodging and vivid recollections of the *luta*, the struggle. I thank Liliane Robacher for fond memories of Curitiba and for her lively company during my time there.

In the United States, thanks to Marianne Schmink for her helpful reading of the manuscript. Every manuscript should have such a conscientious reader. I am also indebted to all the scholars listed in the bibliography from whom I have learned so much. Thanks also to the staff in the office of research services at Loyola University for their essential assistance, and to my department chair, Professor Wiley Feinstein, for his friendship and consistent support of my scholarship and teaching. Jim Lance of Kumarian has been a delight to work with and has offered excellent guidance throughout the publication process. Erica Flock in production has done likewise, and it has been a real pleasure working with them both. I have long been a fan of Kumarian Press, now more than ever.

My husband Bill Heyck read and reread; listened endlessly; offered help, constructive criticism, and encouragement throughout; and has always been the most ardent believer in *Schools in the Forest*. Hands down, he wins the greatest indebtedness award.

Many voices and influences in Brazil and the United States have converged in this story, but I alone am responsible for its errors, including those in translation. ༯

Preface

This is a story of popular empowerment. In particular, it is the story of Projeto Seringueiro (Project Rubber Tapper), a radical educational and political experiment that developed from the ground up in Xapuri, Acre, in Brazil's far western Amazon. Despite overwhelming obstacles, Projeto Seringueiro brought literacy to seringueiros and helped them claim their political rights as citizens, preserve their culture, and defend their forest habitat. In the process, Project Rubber Tapper inspired reformers, not just in Xapuri or Acre, but outside the region as well. Thus, the history of Projeto Seringueiro is a success story, one that resonates far beyond the rainforest.

This book seeks both to narrate the history of Projeto Seringueiro (1981–2008) and to give voice to its principal actors, to allow them to tell their own stories. It means to explain how the rubber tappers and their allies managed to succeed as well as they did despite ferocious opposition from logging and ranching interests that threatened their forest home and their very lives. Though the Projeto Seringueiro experience is a unique response to specific circumstances, many of its features are universally applicable; thus, the Conclusion of this book draws some lessons for those interested in social movements, education, religion, environmental history, and the changing role of NGOs in each. The Projeto Seringueiro example is of particular interest to those NGOs that are currently struggling to create a new identity and role for themselves in locales where progressive, socially responsible governments have come into office.

Projeto Seringueiro began in a traditionally impoverished, oral culture as one important aspect of a broad effort by rubber tappers to become numerate and literate in order to free themselves from economic exploitation by landowners and middlemen, and from the depredations of loggers, ranchers, and speculators who poured into the Amazon during the land rush that began in the mid-1960s. In addition to these challenges, the project faced a chronic lack of funds, trained teachers, and staff. Despite the hostile atmosphere, inauspicious beginnings, and a history of illiteracy among the rubber tappers, Projeto Seringueiro proved tenacious and effective, eventually winning three UNICEF awards and educating several thousand children and adults along the way. Many of its former students, teachers, and coordinating team members have gone on to pursue university degrees and to attain positions of prominence at the local, state, and even national levels. In 1981 illiteracy in rural Acre, which includes Xapuri, stood at nearly 100%; very few forest people even knew how to hold a pencil, much less write their name. By 2008, however, things had changed dramatically: adults and children were taught to read and write, teachers were trained, and new curricula were designed. Thus, by October 2008 the official endpoint of Projeto Seringueiro, when the eight remaining Projeto Seringueiro schools were handed over to the state in a special ceremony honoring the Project's contributions, Projeto Seringueiro had brought about education for empowerment for the rubber tappers of Acre.

Projeto Seringueiro represents nothing less than a turning of tables: a consciousness-raising educational and political revolution. Traditionally, basic education in Brazil has been ineffectual, irrelevant, and accessible largely to urban middle and upper classes. Projeto Seringueiro presents a sharply contrasting model: an effective, relevant, accessible education for political participation by disenfranchised rural populations. It completely inverts Brazil's official educational paradigm, turning it upside down in order to empower the poor, who constitute the majority of the population of Acre and Brazil as a whole. Projeto Seringueiro was closely integrated with the seringueiros' way of life, and was created by seringueiros and their advocates working in partnership. Indeed, one key to Projeto Seringueiro's success has been its openness to cooperation with other groups and individuals to help secure the seringueiros' educational objectives. This quality was most dramatically exemplified by the rubber tappers' remarkable leader, Chico Mendes, who played a crucial but little-known role in Projeto Seringueiro at the same time as he famously mobilized the rubber tappers through their union and worked with environmental organizations.

Traditionally, the rubber tappers' "school" was the rainforest itself. The natural world taught them vital lessons every day, and those lessons were handed down within families for many generations. One way to understand Projeto Seringueiro is to see that the project's founders transformed this natural and informal education into a formal system with schools, teachers, and a curriculum, so the people of Acre would retain their intimate relationship with their habitat while learning skills necessary to survive in a more modern culture and globalized economy. Most urgently, Projeto Seringueiro helped enable seringueiros to mobilize effectively to defend themselves from coerced eviction by ranchers and land speculators.

This book argues that Projeto Seringueiro is best understood when placed within three different contexts: (1) economic globalization; (2) the political struggle in Acre between loggers and ranchers on the one hand, and the forest people on the other; and (3) the intellectual ferment of the 1970s and 1980s. The complete history of Projeto Seringueiro has not been told before, nor has it been presented within these contexts. Moreover, this book shows how four powerful, interrelated intellectual currents informed the work of Projeto Seringueiro's leaders and participants as they coped with the intersection of these contexts. These formative intellectual influences were: (1) popular education along the lines advocated by renowned Brazilian educator Paulo Freire; (2) liberation theology, in particular the Christian base communities; (3) Marxism, or rather, the categories of social analysis used by Marxists; and (4) environmentalism, which is woven into the fabric of the entire story. Given the nature of the contexts, these intellectual influences proved to be remarkably effective. Hence, this book illuminates, among other things, how ideas work in practice.

Another purpose of the book is to give voice to the ordinary people of Acre themselves—in particular, residents of the Xapuri municipality where most of Projeto Seringueiro's activities unfolded—because they are the ones who have turned the tables. They have driven the movement at every stage. Therefore, after several chapters setting out the history and contexts of Projeto Seringueiro, the second part of the book consists of the testimony of the people themselves in interviews gathered over a three-year period. Since most participants in Projeto Seringueiro were simultaneously involved in a wide variety of activities, such as the Union of Rural Workers (Sindicato de Trabalhadores Rurais, STR)— that is, rubber tappers' union—or Christian base communities, their voices illustrate the entwined influences of the period as they were experienced in individual lives. Thus, the book offers proof that people even at the bottom of the social ladder, working in cooperation with other practical idealists and reformers, can create social institutions that radically improve their lives and, through their example, the lives of others beyond their borders.

The history of Projeto Seringueiro encompasses many additional stories: for example, the story of how a liberating education can help bring about personal empowerment and social change; the story of how individuals in partnership create a social movement that no one of them could have done alone, but without each one of them it would not have happened; and the story of how the alternative and subversive can become institutional and official, and the challenges inherent in that process. This study tells these stories and more.

Throughout, *Schools in the Forest* illustrates both the precarious, impecunious existence of grassroots organizations and their sometimes inspiring achievements. Success for Projeto Seringueiro, however, brought about new challenges and caused old fissures and tensions to surface as Projeto Seringueiro leaders grappled with the unanticipated challenges of success. Thus, *Schools in the Forest* is not only many stories, but also a cautionary tale for NGOs: be careful what you wish for, because you might get it. As such, the book will be instructive to students in the classroom and to NGO practitioners in the field, from Bolivia to Bangladesh, who may wish to replicate or adapt to their circumstance certain aspects of Projeto Seringueiro's successes, while avoiding its pitfalls. 🎋

Schools in the Forest

Part I
History

Brazil.

1

Acre:
Land, People and Struggle

The State of Acre

Natural home to jaguars, caimans, anacondas, and piranhas, Brazil's vast Amazon region has long represented the ultimate in mystery and exoticism. Alternately viewed as green hell or paradise on earth, the Amazon evokes different images for different people. To the modern urbanite, it signifies all that is primitive and backward; to the environmentalist, it is the endangered life support system of the planet; to the adventurer, it represents a last frontier; and to the Brazilian government, it suggests an empty expanse whose development provides an escape valve for population pressures elsewhere and exports for lucrative foreign markets.[1]

Acre

To the seringueiros, or rubber tappers, of Acre, the Amazon is home. They travel its river highways, construct their houses from its palm trees, and nourish themselves from its bounty. Acre, known as the "green state" because of the forest, is also environmentally green because the forest peoples' footprint in their habitat is light, and their interaction with the natural world is intimate. They know the importance of striking a delicate balance between human activity and environmental sustainability because they are acutely aware of their dependence on their surroundings.

Acre borders Peru to the west, Bolivia to the south, and the Brazilian states of Amazônia and Rondônia to the north and east. Population

Photo by author.

Rio Acre.

density is very low in Acre, with only about 664,000 inhabitants in its 153,149.9 square miles. It is the largest rubber producer in Brazil, contributing the highest grade of latex, the prized Acre fina. Tropical rainforests cover 93% of its territory, providing for a traditional forest economy of extractive activities.[2] The most recent and innovative commercial activity in Acre is the establishment of a $20 million condom factory by the federal government in 2008 in the town of Xapuri. It is expected to provide badly needed jobs and income for the area and to help in the fight against AIDS in Brazil.[3] The population of Acre is 65% mixed origin, with a Caucasian population of about 26%, 6.8% black, and a minuscule indigenous population of 0.7%. Nearly one-half of the state's residents now live in the capital city of Rio Branco, population 290,639, the result of increasing migration begun in the 1960s and of the expansion of the state and industrial sectors. Public works and beautification campaigns begun by former mayor Jorge Viana in the 1990s and continued through successive administrations have transformed the once dismal city into one with attractive places to visit, though slums

Condom factory [handwritten margin note]

along the river and periphery still serve as intake centers for new migrants and breeding grounds for diseases like malaria. Infant mortality in Acre is an elevated 29 per 1,000 live births. It has always been high in Acre, and it is still common for parents to refer to their "living children." Even today, medical care in the rainforest is rudimentary at best.

Literacy rates for Acre are notoriously unreliable, primarily because there are no recent official statistics for rural areas in the Amazon states where access is difficult; therefore, literacy figures for Acre apply only to Rio Branco and several municipalities such as Xapuri, Brasiléia, and Sena Madureira. Suffice it to say that, though Acre's official illiteracy rate has been estimated at an unrealistic 16%, in the rubber estates, it was virtually 100%, until the advent of more educationally oriented state governments and the work of Projeto Seringueiro in providing basic literacy, as we shall soon discover.[4]

The Educational Context

Education in Brazil has historically been the province of the urban middle and upper classes. Although the federal constitution of 1988 gave considerable autonomy to the municipalities, allowing them to organize their own educational systems and curricula, nothing much happened anywhere in Brazil until 1995, when the federal government made basic education a priority. The Fund for the Development of Fundamental Education and Enhancement of the Teachers' Profession (Fundef) went into effect in 1996 and guaranteed that, for 10 years, 15% of fiscal revenues of states and municipalities must be spent only on elementary education.[5] This fund significantly broadened access to basic education and helped reduce gross regional imbalances.

However, the fact remains that until the end of the twentieth century, Brazil had not established universal access to elementary education. Problems of access, retention, and success at school were and are directly related to the income inequality and regional disparities that characterized the delivery of education in Brazil throughout the twentieth century. The Amazon and Northeast regions have the lowest average income levels and the highest poverty rates in the country, as well as the weakest educational systems. Poverty levels are strongly related to illiteracy rates, which in these areas are about double those for the much richer South

Photo by author.

Logging in Acre.

and Southeast regions.[6] Regional disparities between the rural North/
Northeast and urban centers are huge; for example, the 1980 primary
school census showed that in the Northeast nearly 50% of all children
had never been to school. By contrast, the rate in the urban Southeast
was 10%.

The unequal distribution of income, land, and political power forces
children and adults into the workforce, not the classroom. Moreover,
ongoing problems of low school quality, poor teacher training, and clien-
telism among teachers and administrators complicate the educational
picture.[7] Fundef and subsequent educational reforms have made a big
difference in opening up access, but these improvements are recent; func-
tional illiteracy in Brazil remains high, particularly in states like Acre. It
is not surprising, then, that in the remote rainforest, education had simply never been an option, or even a thought.

For this reason, the advent of Projeto Seringueiro: Cooperative, Education, and Health in 1981 represented a truly revolutionary turning

of the tables. In order to appreciate its full meaning, it is helpful to set the historical, economic, and political context that produced it.

The Move to Develop the Amazon

The centerpiece of the context is the aggressive development policy for the Amazon pursued by Brazil's military government (1964–85). From the beginning, the government urged occupation of the Amazon on a large scale, with propaganda claiming "a land for people, for a people without land." New roads made possible the influx of destitute migrants, while fabulous government incentives made investment irresistible to financiers in the South. Investors jumped at the subsidized loans, corporate income tax exemptions, and tax credits that the government dangled before them.[8] Forests began to succumb to the chainsaw and tractor in the 1960s with the first road projects, which created a swath of destruction and unleashed an uncontrolled flood of migration that escalated massively during the 1970s and 1980s. The clearing and burning of the rainforest left the poor soil exposed and dry. Between the smoldering remains of trees, settlers tried to eke out a living, but with each year the barren earth yielded less, forcing families to move on, repeating the cycle.

However meretricious its effects, uncontrolled immigration did not cause the worst destruction; cattle ranching, which arrived in the 1970s, claims that dubious distinction. Ranching was especially damaging in Acre, where the majority of the invaders were not the landless but large landholders and speculators.[9] Indebted former rubber barons, long weakened by changes in the global market for rubber, were only too happy to sell out to aspiring ranchers and rid themselves of their unprofitable albatrosses. Seeking relief from their bank creditors, many rubber estate owners sold out at low prices.

Beginning in the early 1970s, land sales were aggressively promoted by the state's governor, Wanderley Dantas, a passionate advocate of cattle ranching who virtually gave land away, with one hectare (2.471 acres) going for practically nothing, or "the price of a banana" in local parlance.[10] Speculators rushed to take advantage of the giveaway, holding onto their purchases until prices soared, then selling, without ever intending to develop the land. By 1977 prices had skyrocketed, with one hectare selling for 2,000 cruzeiros. By 1978, 80% of Acre's land was in the hands of large landholders and conglomerates, national and international.[11]

The ranchers cleared the forests of Acre of millions of tons of valuable hardwood, such as mahogany and cedar. These were either exported by logging concerns or simply left to burn. In their drive to accumulate vast estates, ranchers and loggers alike hired pistoleiros to help them expel tappers and subsistence farmers, and to eliminate those who resisted. The demographic dislocation for the seringueiros was enormous, as thousands fled the forest for the city. A study of heads of household in Rio Branco in 1978 revealed that only 13.3% had actually been born in Rio Branco; the others were recent immigrants from the *seringais* (rubber estates).[12]

Yet capital penetration in Acre did not occur in so-called empty areas, but in locales that had been occupied continuously for many generations by seringueiros, who had never had any concept of private property in land. Their notion of "rights" amounted to usufruct—use rights. The interests that motivated the businesspeople, speculators, loggers, and ranchers from the South were alien to the needs and social organization of the forest peoples. The invaders were not interested in the extraction of rubber, and as the former seringais were rapidly transformed into pastures, clashes over the possession of land became aggravated. The migratory flux from country to city increased with the substitution of cattle for people.[13]

By the logic of the speculators, it was necessary to expel the resident labor force so that the land would not depreciate in value. It was also necessary in order to guarantee the ranchers' de facto ownership and remove claims of squatters' rights. Moreover, cattle raising activities required few work hands, so the ranchers could also rationalize expulsions on pragmatic grounds. The new clash, between modern concepts of labor and land usage on the one hand, and traditional work relations and views of nature on the other, was harsh, abrupt, and traumatic for the rubber tappers. Their situation was becoming intolerable: they either had to fight back or face erasure, for the forces arrayed against them were formidable. The rancher and the logger represented larger, faceless, even global, factors—an authoritarian national elite, transnational corporations, and the unfettered flow of capital across national boundaries. For those who favored the economic integration of Acre into the worldwide market for lumber and cattle, human rights violations, environmental depredation, and cultural extinction were an unfortunate, but unavoidable, price to pay for progress.

Defense of the Forest

Yet from the 1970s the seringueiros organized, raised up local leaders, fought for their rights, acquired a political consciousness, revitalized dormant cultural values, and began to seek political alliances. They worked to diversify their economic base, form cooperatives, value education through Project Rubber Tapper, and seek incorporation into the modern world on their own terms.

The seringueiros were assisted by the effective work of numerous groups and individuals, first among them the Catholic Church in Acre, where liberation theology found one of its strongest expressions in Latin America. In the early 1960s, the church in Acre began laying the groundwork for Christian base communities, small groups of neighbors who met regularly to discuss Bible readings and apply them to their own lives and their social and economic situation. Base communities proved to be the key to creating a critical political consciousness among the seringueiros and preparing local leaders to represent and defend the community. They grew like wildfire during the 1970s. The number of monitors (group leaders) increased from 34 in 1971 to 800 in 1978.[14] The base communities and the church's popular radio program *Todos Somos Irmãos* (We Are All Brothers and Sisters), begun in 1973, worked hand in hand; between them, they reached practically every forest community in Acre.

The radio program, the bishop's regular radio broadcasts, and the base community meetings took on special importance because there were no other means for making uncensored information available to the people of Acre. Thus, early on, girded by the social gospel, the church in Acre adopted an adversarial stance vis à vis the federal and local governments.

The driving force behind the church's courageous leadership role in Acre during this period was Dom Moacyr Grechi, bishop of the Prelacy of Acre and the Upper Purús, from 1972 to 1998, and later archbishop of Rondônia. Under Dom Moacyr's intellectual and spiritual direction, the church extended sanctuary to seringueiros fleeing persecution, protected the fledgling union, denounced the perpetrators of violence, reported human rights violations, created a human rights commission, and offered legal assistance through the nationwide Pastoral Land Commissions (CPT), established in 1975, with Dom Moacyr as one of its founders and presidents.[15] At the same time, the church worked assiduously to help the seringueiros develop their own local leadership. As a result of the bishop's example, the message of the base communities, the broadcasts, and the intense effort to train base community monitors, a sense of empowerment gradually began to replace the seringueiros' incapacitating passivity and sense of helplessness.

In the beginning, the church and the rural workers' unions were completely identified with each other, for the unions first arose in the base communities. In fact, it was common practice for union meetings to begin with the Lord's Prayer. By conservative estimate, 70% of the unions were organized from the beginning with the help of the base communities.[16] Gradually, the unions became autonomous, but for many years they maintained a very close relationship with the church.

The most famous of these unions, the Xapuri Rural Workers' Union (STRX), was founded in 1975 by Chico Mendes, the leading figure and international symbol of the seringueiros' resistance movement. His murder by ranchers in 1988 galvanized worldwide opinion and forced the Brazilian government to honor its commitment to the creation of extractive reserves, protected areas for extractivists. Mendes's leadership of the seringueiros' resistance was crucial both to the union and to Project Rubber Tapper, for which he was constantly urging more schools and teacher training. Honest, good-humored, and outgoing, Mendes was instinctively trusted by others. He himself was a rubber tapper who had grown up in the Cachoeira seringal in Xapuri where his father had settled after coming to Acre from the Northeast as a rubber "soldier"—that is, one who "enlisted" to produce rubber for the Allied war effort. Mendes learned to read and write as a young adult from old newspapers provided him by the socialist recluse Euclides Fernandes Távora, who also imparted to Mendes a sense of class struggle and the need for workers to unite. This message was reinforced by the church-sponsored leadership classes that Mendes attended, where themes of brotherhood and solidarity strengthened his innate sense of justice.

Chico Mendes and Son Sandino.

Mendes quickly developed the skills and coherent political consciousness necessary to assume a larger role. He worked closely with fellow union organizer Wilson Pinheiro, who was murdered in 1980 at the union office in Brasiléia for his organizing activities. Pinheiro is credited with having begun the strategy of the *empate* (nonviolent standoff) during the 1970s. Mendes and others refined the empate until it became the most dramatic and effective means of uniting public opinion behind the seringueiros. Other local leaders, all of them rubber tappers, who took up the struggle after Pinheiro's death include Júlio Barbosa, later mayor of Xapuri; Marina Silva, later federal deputy and minister of the environment (2002–2008); and Raimundo de Barros, later city councilman of Xapuri and state representative.

Mendes described the empates as "born of necessity," something "that we created together, from our own heads," and modified "day by day."[17] In an empate, men, women, and children would link arms or lie down in the path of chainsaws and tractors, beseeching operators, often ex-seringueiros like themselves, to cease and sometimes offering to pay their salary. The seringueiros, on their part, were nonviolent, but they were often met with force, as the ranchers would typically call out the police as well as their own armed guards. Tensions mounted and reprisals were fierce as seringueiros escalated the intensity of their empates during the 1980s at the Nazaré, Filipinas, and Equador seringais, and the Bordon ranch, among others. Between 1975 and 1989, the tappers of Brasiléia and Xapuri carried out 45 empates. They won 15 and lost 30; however, according to Mendes, the effort was worth it because "our resistance saved more than 1,200,000 hectares of forest."[18]

As repression from the ranchers increased during the 1970s, seringueiros needed a mechanism for protecting themselves from violence. Mendes and his allies determined that it would strengthen the seringueiros' organization if they joined the new Workers Party (Partido dos Trabalhadores, PT). In a letter to Wilson Pinheiro, shortly before Pinheiro's murder, Mendes describes the urgency of the situation: "Things in Xapuri are really hot. . . . The ranchers had a meeting and they are saying that the only way out for them is to kill the president of the syndicate, the delegate from CONTAG [rural labor federation], Chico Mendes, the padres, and other syndicate delegates." Mendes moved quickly to create the Acre branch of the Workers Party in 1981 and thus link the rubber tappers to a national political structure.[19]

The cause of the seringueiros received a huge boost in 1985 at the first National Encounter of Amazonian Rubber Tappers (Encontro Nacional de Seringueiros da Amazônia) held in Brasília. The meeting was the brainchild of several individuals, including Mendes, anthropologist Mary Allegretti, Oxfam's Tony Gross, and organizer/educator Manoel Estébio Cavalcante da Cunha, all of whom encouraged the seringueiros to link their plight to that of the rainforest itself. Thus they joined with environmentalists, human rights advocates, Indian rights activists, and ordinary citizens worldwide who were alarmed at the ever increasing burning of the forest. At the Encontro, the tappers themselves first put forward the idea of extractive reserves as an alternative to deforestation.

One hundred fifty rubber tappers attended the meeting, many of whom had never before traveled outside their native seringal. Another world awaited them in Brasília. There, they were met not only by representatives from the ministries of Industry and Commerce, Education, Health, Agriculture, Agrarian Reform and Culture, and members of the National Congress, but also by the gleaming, futuristic skyscrapers of the other Brazil, previously unknown to them. The Encontro was a watershed moment in the social construction of environmental policy in the Amazon. We return to the Encontro later, for not only does it illustrate the environmental consciousness and political savvy of the seringueiros, but it also reveals the connection between social justice and environmental policy, and it shows the effectiveness of Projeto Seringueiro in educating local leaders to articulate convincingly both the rubber tappers' plight and their proposals.

From about 1985 Mendes and the seringueiros began working closely with foreign allies, including North American environmentalists and lobbyists critical of international lending institutions for failing to take into account the environmental and social impacts of the Amazon projects they funded.[20] U.S. environmentalists, who were pressing Congress to stop funding risky development projects, welcomed alliance with the rubber tappers because they needed to demonstrate to Congress that there were actually people living in the rainforest whose lives and culture were being destroyed. For their part, the seringueiros needed the international influence of outside organizations to wake up Brazilians and their government.

Meanwhile, the situation in Acre was becoming more dangerous. In 1988, two young seringueiros were shot and wounded during the empate at the Equador estate, and prominent seringueiro leader and base community monitor Ivair Higino was brutally murdered. The Brazilian federal government, fearing further hostilities, agreed in 1988 to establish the first three extractive reserves, among them the bitterly contested Cachoeira reserve, Mendes's home seringal. This was a great triumph for Chico Mendes and his collaborators. Mendes describes the reserves as the idea of "a group of companions committed to faith and idealism."[21] It was also a victory for the North American, European, and Brazilian allies who had been advising and assisting in the struggle.

According to Mary Allegretti, one of the chief architects of the extractive reserves, their great accomplishment was the combination of development with environmental protection. The principal objectives of the extractive reserves, outlined at the 1985 Encontro, included, in addition to allowing seringueiros to live undisturbed in the forest, agrarian reform, the introduction of new technologies to improve production, and the establishment of adequate educational and health systems.[22] There are currently 13 extractive reserves in Acre alone, the largest of which is the Chico Mendes Extractive Reserve, covering 976,570 hectares.

Two months after his victory, Mendes was assassinated in his own home. His murder was deplored throughout the world, and the Brazilian government acted quickly to bring charges against those responsible, Darli Alves da Silva and his son Darci, former owners of the disputed Cachoeira, Mendes's home seringal. Though the two were convicted of murder, they have served time on and off since their convictions. Mendes's assassination, however, was a disaster for the ranchers. As Allegretti points out in her dissertation, it had the effect of revealing to outsiders an important aspect of the environmental question in the Amazon—the conflict over land rights. Mendes's death highlighted the character of the struggle for the defense of the environment in countries like Brazil, where it is bound up with the "concomitant quest for social equity."[23] Allegretti observes that, with the creation of the extractive reserves, sustainable and socially just development became established as the goal, not just for Brazil, but for all developing countries.

A rubber tappers' cooperative, which had first been attempted in the early 1980s, was now reborn under the aegis of the National Rubber Tappers' Council (CNS), after the proposal to create extractive reserves had gained momentum. The cooperative was an attempt to improve the economic condition of the rubber tappers; by working together they could diversify their production, market their rubber and Brazil nuts, and buy goods in bulk at wholesale prices. Cooperatives have a very spotty history, and it was difficult to convince rubber tappers to join. Proponents of the cooperative eventually recruited skeptical extractivists by explaining that, in exchange for a nominal monthly fee for services rendered, the cooperative would enable tappers to increase their income, live sustainably, and preserve the forest. Gradually, the concept took hold, and today there are cooperatives in Xapuri, Brasiléia, Sena Madureira, and other municipalities. Of course, seringueiros are still dependent on the international market. Thus, the 300 to 350 members of the Xapuri cooperative have had to diversify, planting pupunha, guaraná, and cupuaçu to vary their production. Only about 30% of Xapuri's seringueiros have joined the cooperative, and they now shuttle back and forth between barter and the global economy, inserting themselves into the latter insofar as possible and only on conditions that favor sustainability.

Today, national and international entities, both governmental and nongovernmental—such as Oxfam; World Wildlife Federation; Amnesty International; Cultural Survival; Environmental Defense; the Brazilian NGO PESACRE (Grupo de Pesquisa e Extensão em Sistemas Agroflorestais do Acre [Research Extension Group in Agroforesty Systems of Acre]), which received its initial support from the University of Florida; the Brazilian government's research organization EMBRAPA (Empresa Brasileira de Pesquisa Agropecuária [Brazilian Agricultural Research Enterprise]); the CTA (Amazonian Workers Center); CUT (Central Única de Trabalhadores [Workers Central Union]); GTA (Grupo de Trabalho Amazônico [Amazonian Work Group]), and others too numerous to mention, assist seringueiros and native populations in their efforts to diversify their production. Such organizations have helped traditional populations adjust to a new economic reality while preserving their way of life.

However, none of these organizations were in place when the seringueiros' troubles first began. Thus, the rubber tappers' story shows us that threatened communities can organize, form alliances, and advocate on their own behalf. In the trajectory of empowerment, no tool has been more important than that of literacy.

Notes

1. For more on the mystery, meanings, and images of the Amazon, see John Hemming, *Tree of Rivers: The Story of the Amazon* (London: Thames and Hudson, 2008); Kenneth Maxwell, *Naked Tropics: Essays on Empire and Other Rogues* (London and New York: Routledge, 2003); Candice Millard, *The River of Doubt: Theodore Roosevelt's Darkest Journey* (New York: Broadway Books, 2005); Darlene J. Sadlier, *Brazil Imagined: 1500 to the Present* (Austin: University of Texas Press, 2008); and Candace Slater, *Entangled Edens: Visions of the Amazon* (Berkeley, Los Angeles, London: University of California Press, 2002).

2. Instituto Brasileiro de Geografia e Estatística (IBGE), 2007; www.ibge .gov.br.

3. *Guardian Weekly,* April 18, 2008. IDBAmérica, May 4, 2008; www.iadb .org/idbamerica/index.cfm?thisid=3861.

4. IBGE, 2007. Luiz Antônio Pinto de Oliveira, *O Sertanejo, o Brabo e o Posseiro* (*Os cem anos de andanças da população acreana*) (Rio Branco: Universidade Federal do Acre [UFAC], 1985), 33, 35, 84.

5. Japan Bank for International Cooperation, *JBIC Sector Study Series 2004,* No. 2: "Sector Study for Education in Brazil," November 2005, 12.

6. Ibid., 46.

7. Literacy Exchange, World Resources on Literacy, UNESCO, June 6, 2005, pp. 6, 7; http://www1.uni-hamburg.de/UNESCO UIE/literacyexchange/brazil/.

8. Andrew Revkin, *The Burning Season: The Murder of Chico Mendes and the Fight for the Amazon Rain Forest* (New York: Penguin, 1990), 105. See also Marianne Schmink and Charles H. Wood, *Contested Frontiers in Amazonia* (New York: Columbia University Press, 1992); Mauro William Barbosa de Almeida, *Rubber Tappers of the Upper Juruá River, Brazil* (diss., University of Cambridge, England, 1992), 40, 47–48; Maria do Perpétuo Socorro Silva, José Rodrigues Arimatéia, and Frankcinato da Silva Batista, *Seringueiros, Memória, História e Identidade,* vol. 1 (Rio Branco: UFAC, Centro de Documentação e Informação Histórica, CIDH, 1997), 180–82; Barbara Weinstein, *The Amazon Rubber Boom, 1850–1920* (Stanford, CA: Stanford University Press, 1983), 23–24, 267; Warren Dean, *Brazil and the Struggle for Rubber: A Study in Environmental History* (Cambridge: Cambridge University Press, 1987); Amós D'Avila de Paulo, Angela Maria Gomes Alves, Caticilene Rodrigues, Rosilene da Silva, and Valcidene Soares Menezes. "Soldados da Borracha de Xapuri: Memórias de um Viver,: *Xapurys* 1 (Rio Branco: UFAC/DH, 1995), 9, 14.

9. L. Oliveira, *O Sertanejo,* 50–51.

10. Aldenir Rodrigues Mota, Alzenite de Araújo Verçosa, Cosmo Araújo e Araújo, Rosineide Rodrigues Lopes, Zairinéia Soares de Lima, Zilah Carvalho Mastub de Oliveira, "Empate pela Vida e Defesa da Floresta em Xapuri," *Xapurys* 2 (Rio Branco: UFAC, 1996), 7.

11. L. Oliveira, *O Sertanejo,* 52–53.

12. Ibid., 38.

13. Ibid., 57, 38.

14. Maria Ronizia Pereira Gonçalves, "A Fala Sagrada e Social do 'Todos Somos Irmãos' de 1976 a 1982" (BA thesis, UFAC, 1997), 35.

15. Maxwell, *Naked Tropics,* 224.

16. Gonçalves, *Fala Sagrada,* 32, 37.

17. Mota et al., "Empate," 10, 15. For a personal memoir of the entire struggle, see Gomercindo Rodrigues, *Walking the Forest with Chico Mendes: Struggle for Justice in the Amazon,* trans. Linda Rabben (Austin: University of Texas Press, 2007), with Introduction by Biorn Maybury-Lewis.

18. Chico Mendes, *Fight for the Forest: Chico Mendes in His Own Words,* trans. Chris Whitehouse, additional material Tony Gross, ed. Duncan Green

(London: Latin American Bureau, 1989), 79. Adapted from *O Testamento da Floresta,* ed. Cândido Grabowski (Rio de Janeiro: FASE, 1989).

19. Aldenir Rodrigues Mota, Alzenite de Araújo Verçosa, Cosmo Araújo e Araújo, Maria Mavy Dourado de Souza, Rosineide Rodrigues Lopes, Zairnéia Soares de Lima, Zilah Carvalho Mastub de Oliveira, "A Formação do Partido dos Trabalhadores em Xapuri: Os 15 Anos do PT," *Xapurys* 1 (1995): 21–22, 23.

20. Revkin, *Burning Season,* 180–81, 184, 188–89. For more on the environmentalists' efforts, see Pat Aufderheide and Bruce Rich, "Environmental Reform and the Multilateral Banks," *World Policy Journal* 5 (Spring 1988): 301–22. See also David Price, *Before the Bulldozer: The Nambiquara Indians and the World Bank* (Cabin John, MD: Seven Locks Press, 1989).

21. Personal letter from Chico Mendes to Dom Moacyr Grechi, dated July 29, 1987.

22. Mary Helena Allegretti, "Reservas Extrativistas: Parâmetros para uma Política de Desenvolvimento Sustentável na Amazônia," *O Destino da Floresta, Reservas Extrativistas e Desenvolvimento Sustentável na Amazônia,* ed. Ricardo Arnt (Rio de Janeiro: Dumará Distribuidora da Publicações Ltds. Copublished by Instituto de Estudos Amazônicos e Ambientais, Fundação Konrad Adenauer, 1994), 18, 24. In this same volume, see also Mauro William Barbosa de Almeida and Mário Assis Meneses, "Acre—Reserva Extrativista do Alto Juruá," 164–225, and Stephan Schwartzman, "Mercados para Produtos Extrativistas da Amazônia Brasileira," 247–59. For more on extractive reserves, see Mary Allegretti and Stephan Schwartzman, *Extractive Production in the Amazon and the Rubber Tappers' Movement* (Washington, DC: Environmental Defense Fund, 1987). See also Philip M. Fearnside, *Extractive Reserves in Brazilian Amazonia: An Opportunity to Maintain Tropical Rain Forest Under Sustainable Use* (Manaus: National Institute of Amazon Research, October 1988).

23. Allegretti, "Reservas Extrativistas," 18. For more on Chico Mendes's life and death, see Rodrigues, *Walking the Forest.*

2

Lantern in the Forest

Origins, Influences and
Early Years of Projeto Seringueiro

Origins

The inspired idea of a number of individuals, including labor leader Chico Mendes, anthropologist Mary Allegretti, British activist Tony Gross, and ex-seminarian Manoel Estébio Cavalcante da Cunha, whose interview appears in this volume, Projeto Seringueiro began as an adult literacy experiment based on the participatory pedagogy of Paulo Freire. The original purpose of Projeto Seringueiro was to teach seringueiros the basic math and literacy skills necessary to run their cooperative and market their products freely, selling to whomever gave them the best price. Projeto Seringueiro therefore was intended to break the monopoly exercised by the *patrões* (rubber estate owners) and, increasingly, the middlemen who replaced the patrões as they sold out to loggers and ranchers. Projeto Seringueiro did not have as its objective increasing literacy rates in Acre, but rather securing a degree of economic freedom during a time of wrenching dislocation, harsh repression, and social upheaval. Nor was the goal to develop a political consciousness in the oppressed, for the people of Seringal Nazaré, where Projeto Seringueiro began, were already highly mobilized. An acute political awareness was seared into the consciousness of the union members of the seringal, who knew that they were threatened with eviction and ruin, and had to come up fast with an effective way to defend themselves in order to survive. These seringueiros' political skills had been forged in the furnace of the fierce empates of the 1970s, the decade of destruction.

Indeed, Projeto Seringueiro can only be appreciated fully when placed in the context of the *empates* that characterized the period. The most immediate were those in Nazaré and Floresta seringals in 1981, and the protracted *empate* of Santa Fé seringal, which culminated in May 1982, after many months of conflict, in the arrest of 112 seringueiros. Chico Mendes and his cousin Raimundo de Barros, the acknowledged coleader of the movement, and other lieutenants had already received numerous death threats, and the situation was becoming more ominous by the day. Ranchers had burned 1,200 hectares (approximately 3,000 acres), in Santa Fé alone in a period of just a few weeks, far in excess of the requirements of cattle ranching. Such profligate burning was intended to intimidate seringueiros and make it impossible for them to return to the seringal at all. The *empates*, evictions, violence, and the catastrophic cutting and burning of the forest were the topics of urgent union meetings in which Mendes, de Barros, and other members strategized intensely about ways to hold on in the face of the massive assault. After much debate, they determined that their best hope lay in strengthening the Nazaré cooperative, and mounting a strong educational effort in order to make the cooperative work.[1]

Although they knew it was crucial to do so, Mendes and his colleagues found it difficult to strengthen either the union or the cooperative because the long history of exploitation made seringueiros suspicious of alliances, and because they had always worked alone in distant and far-flung *colocações,* or family settlements in the forest. This stubborn reality made it difficult for Mendes, who was urging seringueiros to think of themselves in collective terms, as workers. However, seringueiros were mistrustful even of other seringueiros, and some were on good terms with the middlemen who, unlike the seringueiros, owned burros that facilitated marketing; their favors appealed to tappers who otherwise had to carry their rubber on their backs. Further, middlemen would occasionally help out the seringueiros with a loan or provide them medicine.[2] The middlemen exploited these benefits while also fanning the seringueiros' fears of association, hoping to undermine Mendes's efforts to convince seringueiros to think and act as a cohesive group.[3] Mendes's persistence paid off, however, for it soon became clear to most seringueiros that their cooperative had to grow, and the way to make it grow was to establish a school.

Considering the urgency of their situation, it is quite extraordinary that the seringueiros chose education, a tool that was totally alien to their experience, would take precious time to bear fruit, and that had never before been successfully implemented in the forest. The one forerunner was the noble but ultimately unsustainable effort begun in 1954 by the fiery Italian-born Padre Paolino Baldassari to build church-schools to provide basic literacy to the Indians and seringueiros of the Sena Madureira, not the Xapuri, region.[4] It is also true that marginalized groups in the city, aided by the base communities, were beginning to request schools and medical services, and that syndicates like the one in Xapuri were already raising political awareness.[5] These groups were part of the social movement that was to transform civil society and political culture in Acre in the 1980s. However, in 1981 the social movement (Movimento Social), inspired by liberation theology, the basic tenets of Marxist social analysis, and a growing momentum for a return to democracy, was still very new and active mostly in the city.

To the overwhelming majority of seringueiros in the forest, education had always been for others. It was reserved for people like the manager and the bookkeeper, usually the only ones with the rudiments of literacy and numeracy, for even the rubber estate owner himself was often illiterate. In a completely oral culture, magic seemed to inhere in the inscrutable scribblings of the accounts ledger where the workers' debts were inscribed. The written word was imbued with special properties not intended for forest dwellers—the have-nots—but rather was reserved for the haves and the universe of the city. What's more, written words were a powerful talisman for the seringalista, but they spelled danger for the hapless bumpkin who too often lost his home when he made his "X" in the place marked "undersigned."[6]

Clearly, the decision to build a school in the seringal represented a new way of thinking for the seringueiros, for it meant that they had come to regard basic literacy as a tool in their own liberation, not just a weapon wielded by their oppressors. Taking the school to the forest meant much more than learning a written code; it signaled the possibility of a better future, one the seringueiros would have a hand in creating.[7] It was a risky leap that held both danger and great possibility.

Seringueiros expressed resistance and ambivalence to be sure, for fatalism was deeply ingrained after a century of exploitation and isolation.

Many seringueiros themselves said a school would never work: "*Papagaio velho não pode falar* (You can't teach an old parrot new tricks). . . . No one will ever want to come here and teach us. . . . How will we tend our crops and cut seringa?" But Mendes was an extremely persuasive advocate. Patiently and effectively, he allayed the seringueiros' fears and overcame their doubts. Moreover, he was a seringueiro himself, and he understood the reservations of the local population. Just as important, he possessed a genius for talking, swapping stories, telling jokes, and bringing people together. These talents were essential for bringing reluctant seringueiros on board.

Mendes's immensely influential personal presence and the simple, incontrovertible logic of his argument brought people around to his way of thinking. He directly linked to the rubber tappers' lack of education the monopoly the middlemen enjoyed in marketing. This was an essential connection that had not been made before, for the tappers had always thought that oppression was simply the natural order of things. It had never occurred to them that they themselves could improve their life and conditions of health in the seringais. Relating their economic servitude and precarious existence to the absence of schools represented a tremendous conceptual leap for the seringueiros. Mendes explained to them that the *patrão* (boss) and the middlemen did not want a school because then seringueiros would begin to question their exploitation, and after that the feudal edifice would begin to crumble.

Mendes, who had no formal schooling himself, wanted the seringueiros to think of themselves as a group, as laborers with rights that could be protected by legislation, but only if they themselves acted in concert to make it happen. Further, Mendes repeatedly associated the school with the newborn cooperative, which began operating in March 1982, and in nearly every speech, conversation, and meeting he hammered home the theme that the infant enterprise required literate, numerate workers in order to function. So intimate was the connection between the cooperative and the school, not to mention the chronic need for basic health services, that founding documents were titled "Projeto Seringueiro: Cooperative, Education, and Health for Rubber Tappers of Xapuri-Acre," and the first schools were called "school cooperative."[8]

Besides Mendes himself, who in countless interviews over the years had referred to illiteracy as responsible for the seringueiros' bondage and conception of the world as divided into lords and serfs, the other prime mover behind Projeto Seringueiro in its founding phase was Mary Allegretti, who worked very closely with Mendes from 1981 until his death in 1988.[9] Allegretti had observed firsthand the need for basic literacy when she conducted field research for a master's thesis in Seringal Alagoas several years earlier, and she brought the lessons from that experience with her to Projeto Seringueiro.

Allegretti describes vividly the very first Projeto Seringueiro class, in colocação Já com Fome (Already Hungry), on May 22, 1982, held in a one-room open-sided school constructed from paxiúba palm. Torrential rains poured down for most of the weekend session, flooding pathways and felling groaning trees. A few at a time, rain-soaked, muddy students began arriving, carrying their hammocks and, in homemade rubberized bags, a change of clothes. When the rain let up, they bathed in the nearby forest river, as is the custom, and had dinner. Some had traveled for seven hours and were very hungry. Everyone was given a folder with the *Poronga* text, a pencil, and an eraser. Many had never seen a folder and did not know how to open it. Others began to look through *Poronga* upside down. Class began with a conversation on the title of the book, named for the head lantern that seringueiros wear in order to see in the dark and so free their hands for work. It was a fitting symbol for what the creators of Projeto Seringueiro wished to do: bring the light of learning into the dark forest using the seringueiros' own instrument to illuminate the path.[10]

The overall thrust of *Poronga* itself was popular empowerment. Students discussed the central themes of the seringueiros' organization, their quest for autonomy through the all-important union, the struggle for the land, and the consciousness that they were agents in the construction of a new society. This thinking was influenced by Mendes's firm belief that the union was the seringueiros' best defense.[11] From these topics, some twenty-five "generative" terms, an idea taken from Paulo Freire, were selected for discussion. These included words from the environment, from the seringueiros' daily lives, such as forest, food, hammock, rubber, hunting, kerosene, fever, work; and more political or abstract terms like squatters' rights, cooperative, empate, union, and government.[12] Important throughout was the idea of knowledge, in particular of valuing the seringueiros' knowledge, their life experience, and also the kind of knowledge that they would learn in school. Discussion focused on the traditional system of exploitation, the captive and free seringueiros as Mendes had termed them, and their right to food and health. Conversation included the relationship between nature and culture, and how humans transform nature through their work. In this context, seringueiros were asked to begin reflecting upon what they soon regarded as their life project—that is, to envision their own empowerment.[13]

The strong influence of Paulo Freire was clearly present, and the method was intended in Freireian fashion to respond to two needs: (1) to value the previously denigrated knowledge and universe of the seringueiros, and to use that base to help them reflect critically on their situation in order to transform it; and (2) to learn math, essential for marketing on their own. The math lesson reproduced a ledger account sheet of a company store, based on Allegretti's previous research. Students began to learn what debits, credits, and balances were, as they were initiated in the secrets of basic mathematical operations that unlocked the mystery of their perpetual indebtedness.[14] By the end of the first weekend, all students had learned to write the word *comunidade,* certainly a concept that resonated with many organizers, but the topic that really captured their interest was math, the tool that would help them achieve their economic freedom.[15]

Projeto Seringueiro was the first effort by the first NGO created in Acre, CEDOP-AM (1981–82), which was replaced by the CTA (Amazonian Workers Center) in 1983; Allegretti created both of them. According to her, the conditions that made Projeto Seringueiro possible were (1) the high state of mobilization of Seringal Nazaré; (2) the availability of key people, such as Mendes and Allegretti herself, and also Raimundo de Barros, Ronaldo and Marlete de Oliveira, Manoel Estébio Cavalcante da Cunha, and Dercy Teles, who were among the first teachers; (3) the financial means to make it possible, including a $5,000 interest-free loan from Oxfam in 1981, 10% of which was for education and the rest for the cooperative, and, in 1982, $32,700 from the Brazilian Ministry of Education and Culture (MEC), both secured by Allegretti; and (4) a methodology adapted to conditions in the seringal.[16]

The methodology was crucial to the success of the school. Allegretti obtained technical assistance from internationally respected educator

Sérgio Haddad of the Ecumenical Center for Documentation and Information (CEDI, Centro Ecumênico de Documentação e Informação), a Freireian educational NGO in São Paulo, in applying Freire's principles to the development of the aptly named *Poronga,* the first text.

Influences: Paulo Freire

Who was Paulo Freire? His ideas shaped popular education in Brazil, Latin America, Asia, and Africa through his prolific writing; his teaching at various universities, including Harvard and Texas; and his work with UNESCO. Born in the impoverished northeastern city of Recife, Paulo Freire (1921–1997) experienced hunger as a child. This formative experience motivated him to dedicate himself at an early age to struggle against poverty and oppression. His own childhood taught him firsthand that the dispossessed live in a "culture of silence," and that ignorance and passivity are the result of systemic ills caused by political, economic, and social institutions, including a soul-destroying paternalism that robs the poor of all initiative.

Realizing that the educational system was a major vehicle for perpetuating the culture of silence, Freire turned to adult literacy as a way to promote direct engagement by the poor in their own struggle to liberate themselves and their oppressors in the creation of a more just society. For Freire, liberation was based in love and equality; thus, the oppressed could not liberate themselves only to become oppressors like their patrões. Rather, they had to work to free themselves and their oppressors from the situations that dehumanized them both. Freire melded his eclectic readings of Marx, Sartre, Mounier, Eric Fromm, Louis Althusser, Ortega y Gasset, Mao, Martin Luther King Jr., Che Guevara, Unamuno, and Marcuse into his own authentic formula for liberation.

Basically, Freire's method moves from reflection to praxis and back again, never remaining at either the theoretical or the action end of the pendulum, but always going back and forth between the two in open dialogue based on issues identified by the community. Thus, Freire's method represents a unity of theory and practice; it rests on a respect for the "intellectual universe" or knowledge and lived experience of the student, the raw material for discussion in the "cultural circle." One can imagine what a new concept this was for the seringueiros whose forest culture, way of speaking Portuguese, and local knowledge had been den-igrated or ridiculed for over a century, and who were commonly viewed by their patrões as merely part of the forest's flora and fauna, to be ex-ploited like any other natural resource.

Freire's basic assumption is that humankind's ontological vocation is to be a subject who acts upon his or her world; hence, history is con-text, opportunity, or a problem to be solved, not destiny.[17] The world is dynamic, not static and closed. In acting, humans move toward creating a fuller life and overcoming dehumanizing situations. Freire's method holds that everyone, no matter how oppressed, is capable of engaging in critical dialogue with others and the world.[18] In the process, the word takes on new power, no longer an abstraction or magic, but a means by which individuals discover themselves and their potential. Both the as-sumption and the process are dramatically illustrated in Projeto Serin-gueiro. As Freire puts it, each person wins back one's right to say one's own word, to name the world. An illiterate peasant who participates in this sort of educational experience comes to a new awareness of self, has a new sense of dignity, and is stirred by a new hope. In the process of learning to read, individuals discover that they are creators of culture, and they become subjects acting to change oppressive social structures.

To Freire, there is no such thing as a neutral educational process. Ed-ucation either functions to integrate one into the logic of the oppressive system and perpetuate conformity, or it becomes the practice of freedom, the means by which men and women deal analytically and creatively with reality and transform their world.[19] It was because of the transformative power of consciousness raising that Freire became one of the very first in-tellectuals arrested and exiled by the military government in 1964, in a de-termined campaign to stamp out precisely the kind of critical thinking that the popular teacher was advocating. As Freire always said: literacy is not a pedagogical phenomenon with political implications, but rather a political phenomenon with pedagogical implications.

This was certainly the case with Projeto Seringueiro, where the idea was to stimulate individual and group reflection on problems taken from the seringueiros' environment, and through discussion increase critical problem-solving capacities and community participation while also teaching reading and writing. Thus, it created a politically active, cohesive community absolutely committed to improving the lives of its members and preserving the forest.

Other groups besides Projeto Seringueiro were also active during the 1980s: the Rural Workers Union (STR), established by Chico Mendes and others; the Amazonian Workers Center (CTA) itself, the umbrella NGO for Projeto Seringueiro, which had other social and environmental projects in addition to Projeto Seringueiro; the National Rubber Tappers Council (CNS); and the Christian base communities (CEBs), all of which held similar, overlapping goals and memberships. Projeto Seringueiro was thus part of the ongoing, large-scale political and consciousness-raising social movement that represented broadly based efforts at popular political mobilization by civil society during a period of military dictatorship and its pursuit of economic development at any cost.

In August 1982 Projeto Seringueiro's leadership asked the Ecumenical Center for Documentation and Information (CEDI) to evaluate with them the effectiveness of the *Poronga* text. They met in São Paulo, with Freire himself present, and discussed a number of questions. Chief among them was the fact that Projeto Seringueiro's creators had discovered that, unlike in other literacy programs, the seringueiros showed no interest in discussing the generative word based on familiar themes, the way the Freireian method usually develops a critical consciousness in the students. Instead, the seringueiros wanted to learn the tools of reading, writing, and doing math, not the context that these expressed. The generative terms that were part of the universe of the seringueiro did facilitate the process, but they did not motivate political reflection. What motivated discussion was information about the unknown, life in the city, the technological uses of rubber, and the distant reality of the world beyond the seringal.[20] These and other observations were reflected in the revised materials produced by CEDI shortly afterward, which correlated the text more closely with the actual experience and expressed interests of the seringueiros themselves. In this way, theory was adapted to practice, and the seringueiros clearly took charge of their own education.

In urban areas, salaried workers had the opportunity to reflect on their conditions, while in Projeto Seringueiro the students/rubber tappers were directly involved in the transformation of reality, sometimes at the risk of their lives, and always at the risk of their livelihoods. This circumstance made the school not a place of consciousness raising, for consciousness was already extremely elevated, but rather a site for acquiring skills that could be utilized immediately and that represented the difference between winning and losing everything.[21] It was empowerment in the most basic sense.

Influences: Liberation Theology

Freire's pedagogy, while crucial, was not the only propelling force in the trajectory of empowerment; there were also other dynamic and interdependent factors. Perhaps the best way to appreciate their interconnectedness is to visualize as follows the intellectual construction materials of Projeto Seringueiro's first forest school: Freire's pedagogy serves as the earthen floor; liberation theology, the Marxist-inflected wooden posts; and environmentalism, the palm canopy, or roof.[22] Freire's thought, while foundational, was thus one of several simultaneous, mutually reinforcing components of the structure.

Liberation theology, the school's pillars, is nothing less than a radical engagement of Christianity with the world. As leading exponent Gustavo Gutiérrez puts it, liberation theology views the world from the "underside of history"—that is, from the perspective of the poor, people like the rubber tappers of Acre.[23] This focus is the distinguishing genius of liberation theology, for it links theology to the struggle for justice, much as Freire's pedagogy links education to that same objective. Liberation theology is not a new theology; rather, it is a new way of doing theology that originated in Latin America in the 1950s and that represents a retrieval of the mission of the early church—the egalitarian, communitarian example of the first disciples, and the message of liberation contained in both the Old and New Testaments.

By the 1960s great changes were transforming the churches in Latin America. Most important was the Second Vatican Council (1962–65) and Pope John XXIII's two groundbreaking encyclicals that provided much of the material for discussion at the Council meetings, and that opened the Catholic Church to the world: *Mater et Magistra* (Christianity and Social Progress; May 15, 1961), and *Pacem in Terris* (Peace on Earth; April 11, 1963). These two documents, and the deliberations on their meaning, changed the course of Catholic social thought.[24]

Moreover, they freed Latin American theologians to engage in a thoroughgoing critique of what Gutiérrez termed "developmentalist capitalism," by which he meant an economic practice that builds great wealth for a few, the foreign and native elites, on the backs of the many, those for whom hunger is a daily, crushing reality. In other words, "developmentalism" was an institutional sin that perpetuated social injustice.

By the end of the 1960s the developmentalist model had brought vigorous criticism from Latin American and other sociologists, economists, and theologians. Critiques began to unmask the true cause of underdevelopment—that everything was structured so that benefits flowed to the already developed "center" with nothing left for the "periphery." The poverty of third-world countries was the price to be paid for first-world abundance. The periphery-center relationship had to be replaced, and the theology of development began to give way to a theology of liberation.

Vatican II created the free, critical theological atmosphere that gave Latin Americans the official impetus to think for themselves about their pastoral experience in their own countries, and the overwhelming fact of that experience was poverty. At a meeting of Latin American theologians in Rio de Janeiro in 1964, Gutiérrez described theology as "a critical reflection on praxis in the light of the word of God." There followed many more meetings and lectures on poverty throughout Latin America that acted as laboratories for the Medellín conference of 1968, in which the idea of a theology of liberation was first widely discussed, and where the Latin American bishops denounced "the international monopolies and the international imperialism of capital," as well as the "institutionalized violence" that plagued their countries.[25] By the time of the Puebla conference in 1979, liberation theology was regarded as central to the mission of the church, and at Puebla great attention was devoted to the preferential option for the poor.

Liberation theology rejects both capitalism and socialism in favor of a third way, though it makes use of the basic tools of social analysis provided by Marxism, such as class struggle. Capitalism is universally regarded as oppressive by liberationists because they have seen the results of uncontrolled capitalism in Latin America. Pope John Paul II, hardly viewed as a liberation theologian, defines the root of economic oppression as "the supremacy of capital—enjoyed by the few—over labor—practiced by the many."[26]

The crucial councils and conferences, the economic and political events of the 1960s, and the insights of clergy and lay pastoral agents in Latin America combined to help unify into a movement broadly dispersed activities. In this process, two factors played a very important role: (1) Christian base communities (CEBs), which began as experiments in Brazil and elsewhere with new forms of egalitarian church organization; and (2) "conscientization," Freire's educational method, which soon spread far beyond Brazil.

Not surprisingly, powerful actors, such as church conservatives and military governments, soon came to see base communities and liberation theology as threats not only to church authority, but also to the entire social and political order. Giving voice to the poor represented a radical paradigm shift for the church; as such, it provoked heated controversy, censure, and retributions throughout Latin America. In some places, like El Salvador, Nicaragua, and Brazil among others, those who opted for the poor paid dearly, sometimes with their lives. As Brazilian theologian Leonardo Boff points out, among the poorest of the world, "faith is not only 'also' political, it is above all else political."[27]

Base communities and Paulo Freire's consciousness raising helped the poor come to an awareness of their own dignity and rights; identify the root causes of their oppression; overcome fear and fatalism; and become architects of their own destiny. This is, of course, precisely what Chico Mendes gave his life to achieve for seringueiros through the Xapuri Rural Workers Union (STRX), the cooperative, the Workers Party (PT), the extractive reserves, and Projeto Seringueiro.

Influences: Marxism

One can easily see the interrelatedness of Freireian and liberationist thought, the foundation and supporting posts of our open-sided school. The influence of Marxism, however, is less obvious. It was at best a very vague notion even to most Projeto Seringueiro leaders, but it was also an important analytical tool for an influential few. Certainly, Marxism was in the air during the 1970s and 1980s; heroic images of revolutionary figure Ernesto "Che" Guevara adorned posters and T-shirts and inspired many young reformers throughout Latin America and beyond. Further, Marxist tools, especially the concepts of social class and the oppression of labor by capital, were extremely helpful in structuring and making sense of complex economic and political issues. Clearly, Marxist thought informed the social teaching and mobilization efforts of the priests, nuns, and lay religious workers in Xapuri. Such, however, was not the case for the bishop of Acre, Dom Moacyr. He, like most everyone else, was horrified by the magnitude of human suffering and environmental destruction wrought by unbridled capitalism, which at times required him literally to interpose himself between the seringueiros and their pursuers, and he was relentless in his condemnation of an economic system utterly lacking any ethical base, but he was no Marxist.[28] Nevertheless, for all liberationists, the seringueiros' struggle against the loggers, ranchers, and their gunmen was not only that of David and Goliath, it was also that of exploited workers versus transnational capitalism. Virtually all religious persons, including base community members and Projeto Seringueiro personnel, posed in stark terms the unequal contest between rich and poor, powerful and weak, as it was being played out in the Amazon.

Marxism was popular throughout Latin America during this period, and some of the intellectual lights behind Projeto Seringueiro—notably Chico Mendes himself, who, as labor leader, tended to see the struggle in class terms; and Manoel Estébio Cavalcante da Cunha, and Binho Marques, whose interviews follow—were members of the clandestine Communist Party of Brazil (PCdoB) during the dictatorship. In fact, most members of the Workers Party (PT) were also members of the PCdoB. This is not as radical as it sounds, for going underground was the only way to speak freely and safely during an era of political repression. But, as Marques observes wryly in his interview in Part II of this study, anyone who may have harbored the fantasy of creating a Marxist scenario in the rainforest soon realized the absurdity of trying to impose any kind of dogmatic structure on the independent-minded seringueiro. Even so, long after Marques and da Cunha had quit the PCdoB with the return of democracy to Brazil in 1985, they continued to find Marxist social categories useful analytical instruments. Marques and da Cunha are among what Dom Moacyr terms the "tiny handful" of intellectuals in Acre who have read Marx.[29] Others would include journalists and faculty members at the Universidade Federal do Acre. Marxism was more a mystique than a plan whose élan galvanized many groups involved in the social movement, infusing them with enthusiasm and hope, and inspiring them with the example of Che. These included university students, various urban groups, syndicate and base community activists, and some Projeto Seringueiro leaders and teachers. Marxism was never a fully articulated influence on Projeto Seringueiro; most seringueiros had never heard the term until they were accused of being Marxist subversives for joining the union.

Influences: Environmentalism

The roof that shades our structure is, of course, environmentalism. Though protection of their forest home was the initial expression of the seringueiros' environmentalism, by the mid-1980s under Chico Mendes's direction, Projeto Seringueiro had moved toward full-blown environmentalism through alliances with national and international NGOs. Seringueiros were ecologists by nature in that they knew they depended upon the forest, and had to keep their economic activities well within the recuperative capabilities of the ecosystem. In short, they realized that they were bounded by natural limits. This was a lesson whose truth was brought home to them firsthand every day. It was Chico Mendes's genius for making alliances that brought a more sophisticated type of environmentalism to the forest dwellers and that introduced professional environmentalists to a gold mine of culturally based environmental knowledge. These two different worlds worked together amazingly effectively, thanks to Mendes's unique personal gifts and the inclusive embrace of his leadership style. The Union began to cooperate with NGOs like the Environmental Defense Fund, Rainforest Alliance, and Brazil's EMBRAPA, among others, in order to publicize the plight of the forest populations, halt deforestation, and work for the creation of extractive reserves. From the very beginning, however, sustainable environmental and economic practices were woven into the palm roof of our structure, and provided Projeto Seringueiro's reason for being.

With the entwined influences of Freire's pedagogy, liberation theology, Marxism, and environmentalism, Projeto Seringueiro built a simple, authentic classroom that made the project effective from the outset.

Early Years

To the original school in Seringal Nazaré was added another in Seringal São Pedro, also in 1982. Beginning in 1983, because of the demand for new schools, Projeto Seringueiro's team decided to separate the schools from the cooperative. Soon schools were added in three more seringals: Floresta, Boa Vista, and Santa Fé, all with the same main objective: to teach reading, writing, and accounts in order to master the commercial system.[30] Early on, Projeto Seringueiro began holding intensive workshops to train monitors, as teachers were called at that time, in order to improve the quality of instruction and to enable schools to function with resident teachers from their own areas, not just the original Projeto Seringueiro founders, who were needed to oversee planning for the growing program. The project also created an essential support team in Rio Branco under the aegis of the Amazonian Workers Center (CTA) to produce teaching materials and "accompany" monitors—that is, to supervise, train, mentor, assist, and encourage teachers.

In the highly polarized ideological climate of the 1980s, Projeto Seringueiro tried, with varying degrees of success, to steer an independent course of nonalignment with either the Workers Party (PT)—the Acre branch was founded by Mendes in 1981 and claimed the loyalty of virtually 100% of the seringueiros of Xapuri—or with the Catholic Church, the most intrepid opponent of the dictatorship and defender of the poor. Even so, rumors spread that Projeto Seringueiro was the work of communist padres and professors, that the money for the cooperative came from Russia or Cuba, and that its merchandise came from abroad. None of this was true, though Marxist hues tinged the broad palette of the social movement to varying degrees. Attempting to intimidate members of the cooperative and Projeto Seringueiro, police searched the CTA cooperative on various occasions, but found nothing illegal.

In terms of ideology, Projeto Seringueiro made clear its Freireian, not partisan, underpinnings. These, ironically, were much more subversive than any political party identification could ever have been. The project's leadership affirmed as follows:

1. Political consciousness and organization of workers are not the result of radical speeches against class exploitation as some segments of the left maintained, but rather of a practice directed toward the transformation of the concrete conditions of their lives.
2. The desired transformation should be planned and implemented by the combined contribution of all parties involved under conditions of equal participation; no group is privileged—neither workers nor intellectuals, political or union leaders.
3. There is no baseist mystique of the worker: just because laborers are exploited does not mean that they are always right; nor is there a "vanguardist" tendency, which would regard either intellectuals or popular leaders as directing the process, because it is to be carried out by all in dialogue.
4. Projeto Seringueiro's independence from partisan control and from control by any funding source would be aggressively defended.
5. Projeto Seringueiro's objectives could only be realized through the involvement of full-time professional teachers and administrators, not through political parties or conventional leaders.[31]

These affirmations prepared the way for greater involvement by the civil sector and NGOs, though many in Projeto Seringueiro held out hope that the political climate in Brazil would one day change and that a democratic government in the state of Acre would assume and reproduce Projeto Seringueiro's model.[32] This is in fact what eventually happened, though it seemed a utopian dream in the early years, and when it finally occurred it posed new and unexpected identity issues for the NGO.

Throughout Projeto Seringueiro's history—which unfolded principally, though not exclusively, in the municipality of Xapuri—there existed a symbiotic relationship, not only between the union, the cooperatives, and the schools, but also between the base communities and the schools. Base communities were not only the legitimizing arm of liberation theology, but they were also crucial in mobilizing tappers and other forest peoples, and in shielding them from the violence of the loggers and ranchers. Moreover, the tappers received leadership training from clergy and lay leaders in order to serve as monitors conducting Sunday morning meetings in their homes. This training dovetailed with the education for empowerment offered by Project Rubber Tapper. Seringueiros sometimes moved on to create a school as a result of their often profound base community experiences. At other times, the school itself encouraged communities to reactivate a base community that had become inactive or to start a new one. A study conducted by anthropologist Constance Campbell in São Luis do Remanso in 1988 shows that nine of 13 communities with a Projeto Seringueiro school also had a base community, and of these nine communities, five had monitors with dual roles as teachers and base community monitors.[33] The liberation theology that informed the activities of the base communities offered another opportunity for seringueiros to discuss ways to improve their lives, this time from a faith perspective. The important thing to remember is that the spirit of change grew simultaneously in the base communities, union, cooperative, and the Projeto Seringueiro schools, all of which were intimately interconnected and mutually reinforcing.

All the initial seringueiro cooperatives created in 1981 had failed by 1984, though some have been reconstituted since that time, including the Xapuri cooperative in 1988; the success of the health posts has been uneven at best. However, as Campbell points out, the schools, initially designed solely to support the cooperatives, soon became the "sustaining force in the community" as they took root and grew in the early and mid-1980s.[34] No one would have predicted this turn of events. For example, during the 1988 empate of Cachoeira, seringueiros slept and cooked in the school. The forest schools served as both meeting place and sanctuary, much like the churches, and they have nurtured and strengthened a sense of community. Moreover, conservation has been at the core of all aspects of Projeto Seringueiro, providing the foundation for the entire experience—education for community mobilization in defense of the forest.[35]

In retrospect, one can see that by 1981, Projeto Seringueiro was an idea whose time had come, and for the seringueiro leaders there was no point in waiting around for the state to take the initiative. Basic education in Acre, as in Brazil generally, had historically been a very low priority, neglected by bloated, incompetent, or financially strapped administrations. Though the situation in all states was to improve markedly with the giant push for basic education under Fundef, that program did not even begin until 1996. Meanwhile, for the impoverished state of Acre to turn its attention to basic education was impossible, for the uncontrolled inflation set in motion by the land speculation in the 1970s was followed by neoliberal structural adjustments that required draconian budget cuts, especially in education and health—the wages of economic globalization. Successive waves of evicted and displaced forest peoples overwhelmed Rio Branco's minuscule resources, the unanticipated but predictable result of the federal government's Amazon "development" policy. Who then could mobilize the community if not the community itself?

The opening that began under President Ernesto Geisel (1974–79) had loosened restrictions on the press and permitted more open discussion of public policies. As a result, leftist intellectuals in Rio Branco at the new Federal University of Acre (UFAC), which was opened in 1972, and the influential opposition newspaper *O Varadouro* (the *Forest Path*) which was founded in 1977, began to speak openly about the need to redress social injustices and incorporate the poor majority into the life of the state. As these forces grew, they came to operate much as a firebreak, containing the flames that threatened to engulf the forest. In this context, it is important to understand that Projeto Seringueiro was an extraordinary enterprise: inspired, bold, and born of both hope and desperation.

Projeto Seringueiro differed from all previous responses by seringueiros, their organizations and defenders, in that it was not merely reactive but also proactive, envisioning a better future for the seringueiro and providing the road map for the journey.[36] It was extremely risky because there was absolutely no reason to think it would succeed or that the seringueiro would even want to learn how to read. Paulo Freire himself once suggested that Projeto Seringueiro educators examine their basic assumptions and ask themselves, "Why, in an oral forest seringueiros need to learn to read?"[37] Freire observed th been for the immediate political and economic crisis, Pro probably would have failed at the outset because, in th⌐ ⌐⌐ ⌐ ing was unnecessary and unrelated to the seringueiros' daily life.

Chico Mendes, however, knew that both the immediate need and his vision for the future required schools in the forest. What he could not know was that Projeto Seringueiro, in spite of its many hardships, was to play an even more important role than he had imagined. Not only did it impart the necessary skills for running the cooperative and strengthening the union in the early 1980s, it also played an unforeseen role in equipping seringueiros to articulate their demands at the important first National Encounter of Rubber Tappers in 1985, where the concept of extractive reserves was first publicly laid out by the seringueiros themselves; in producing leaders at the community, state, and even national levels; in influencing both rural and indigenous education throughout Acre; and, most important, in changing the seringueiros' self-concept and worldview, which made all of the above possible. It is, indeed, a story of popular empowerment.

Notes

1. Mary Helena Allegretti, "A Construção Social de Políticas Ambientais: Chico Mendes e o Movimento dos Seringueiros" (PhD thesis, Universidade de Brasília-DF, 2002), 353, 374. Available online at Marina Silva Biblioteca da Floresta, http://www.ac.gov.br/bibliotecadafloresta.

2. Edir Figueira Marques de Oliveira, *Educação Básica no Acre 1962–1983, Imposição política ou pressão social?* (Rio Branco, EFM, 2000) 229.

3. Allegretti, *Construção Social,* 377.

4. E. de Oliveira, *Educação Básica,* 176.

5. Ibid., 159–66.

6. Notes from *Seminário da Poronga,* Poronga Evaluation Seminar with Paulo Freire, São Paulo, August 1982, Archives of CEDOP, Curitiba. Seminar report also available online from Marina Silva Biblioteca da Floresta, http://www.ac.gov.br/bibliotecadafloresta.

7. Allegretti, *Construção Social,* 357.

8. *Seminário da Poronga.*

9. Allegretti, *Construção Social,* 356.

10. Ibid., 360.

11. Ibid., 370.

12. E. de Oliveira, *Educação Básica,* 228. The generative terms in Portuguese were *mata, pato, paca, comida, morada, jirau, jarina, rede, borracha, caça, farinha, querosene, febre, paxiúba, trabalho, seringueiro, and riqueza,* and more political terms such as *posse, cooperativa, empate, sindicato,* and *governo.*

13. Allegretti, *Construção Social,* 370–371.

14. Ibid., 371.

15. Ibid., 373.

16. Ibid., 360.

17. Richard Schaull, Foreword, in Paulo Freire, *Pedagogy of the Oppressed* (New York: Herder and Herder, 1970), 12–13.

18. Ibid., 13.

19. Ibid., 15.

20. Allegretti, *Construção Social,* 317.

21. Ibid., 377.

22. The author is grateful to Hunter Heyck for this illustrative analogy.

23. Alfred T. Hennelly, S.J., *Liberation Theology: A Documentary History* (New York: Orbis, 1990), xvi. For more on liberation theology, see Clodovis Boff, *Deus e o Homem no Inferno Verde: Quatro Meses de Convivência com as CEBs do Acre* (Petrópolis: Vozes, 1980), and *Teologia Pé no Chão,* 2nd ed. (Petrópolis: Vozes, 1984).

24. Hennelly, *Liberation Theology,* 1–2.

25. Ibid., 41.

26. Leonardo Boff and Clodovis Boff, *Introducing Liberation Theology* (New York: Orbis, 1987), 27.

27. Ibid., 39.

28. Denis L. Heyck, *Surviving Globalization in Three Latin American Communities* (Toronto: Broadview Press, 2002), 95–106.

29. Author's interview with Dom Moacyr Grechi, August 10, 2007, Rio Branco, Acre.

30. Allegretti, *Construção Social,* 381.

31. Ibid., 384.

32. Ibid., 387.

33. Constance Elaine Campbell, "The Role of a Popular Education Project in Mobilizing a Rural Community: A Case Study of the Rubber Tappers of Acre, Brazil" (MA thesis, University of Florida, 1990), 103.

34. Ibid., 93.

35. Ibid., 106.

36. Allegretti, *Construção Social,* 358.

37. *Seminário da Poronga.*

3

Disarray,
Renewal and Absorption

Disarray

The heroic, early years of Projeto Seringueiro found their highest expression in the Encontro Nacional de Seringueiros (National Encounter of Rubber Tappers) in 1985 in Brasília, where Projeto Seringueiro's rubber tapper/teachers played a significant role in shaping the debate and articulating the argument for extractive reserves. The idea for the reserves was born in Acre, and spread throughout the Amazon as tappers in the region made common cause for the first time at the Encounter. But storm clouds were already threatening to extinguish Projeto Seringueiro's lantern, for the project suffered from a chronic lack of funds and frequent personnel turnover. In fact, one could say that the high point for the rubber tappers' movement in the Amazon was also, ironically, the low point for Projeto Seringueiro.

In 1985 the state agreed to begin paying Projeto Seringueiro teachers; however, as is often the case in situations where responsibilities are not clearly defined and bureaucracies are lumbering, Projeto Seringueiro schools fell between the administrative cracks. Thus, for a while, neither the state nor the impoverished Projeto Seringueiro supplied salaries and teaching materials, or otherwise administered the schools. At the same time, teacher training in Projeto Seringueiro was more important than ever because the number of schools had jumped from eight to 16 in 1985 in anticipation of the Encounter and the extractive reserves proposal. The growth was totally unplanned, and ill-prepared individuals were accepted as teachers because the need was great.

There was no one in charge in 1985: no oversight, no funds, and virtually no staff. Just as Projeto Seringueiro was about to snatch defeat from the jaws of the Encounter victory, Chico Mendes, who had been involved front and center in pushing for the reserves, strengthening the Rural Workers Union, and forging alliances with environmentalists in Brazil and beyond, turned his attention to the plight of CTA/Projeto Seringueiro. He became disgusted with the state, which he never trusted to honor its commitments in the first place, and impatient with the inaction of the project, whose few remaining members he dismissed.[1]

Mendes brought the young university graduate Arnóbio "Binho" Marques on board in 1986 to resuscitate the CTA/Projeto Seringueiro. Marques, who later became governor and whose interview follows, was a political activist, close friend of Mendes, and a history teacher in the public system. He had given a well-received workshop to Projeto Seringueiro's eight teachers in 1985, before the expansion to 16 schools, and they were eager for him to bring order out of chaos. Though Mendes decried the disarray that resulted from the abrupt increase from eight to 16 schools, he himself was the driving force behind the expansion. His experience was that the state could never be counted on for anything, and he urged the creation of more schools to increase literacy in order to enable greater political participation by seringueiros. He had thus insisted on expanding dramatically the number of schools for all age groups in order to catch the cresting extractive reserve wave for the seringueiros' benefit. The more rubber tappers who were educated—and who could vote, strengthen the union, the Workers Party (PT), and the cooperatives—the more there would be to safeguard both their economic livelihood and the forest. It was decidedly secondary to Mendes that the project could not train teachers as fast as he created schools; to him, this was primarily a political, not an educational, issue.

In addition to Binho Marques, Mendes invited the former seminarian and now educator and organizer Manoel da Cunha to offer an extensive teacher training course early in 1986 that teachers from numerous forest communities attended. This course trained not only the recently hired teachers for the jump from eight to 16 schools but also further increased the supply of teachers in anticipation of the creation of extractive reserves. Shortly afterward, da Cunha left CTA/Projeto Seringueiro for four years (1986–90) to work in Carabarí, in the neighboring state of Amazonas, where he and Dercy Teles began a highly successful literacy program for *caboclo* (racially mixed) riverine populations based on Project Rubber Tapper's model, the first example of the expanding influence of Projeto Seringueiro, even as many still doubted whether the project itself could stage a comeback.

By the time the extractive reserves were officially decreed in 1988, Project Rubber Tapper had mushroomed from eight to 16 to 40 schools, largely due to Mendes's constant urging, and the administrative situation had spiraled totally out of control. When Binho Marques took over as head of CTA/Projeto Seringueiro in 1987, he faced seemingly insurmountable challenges. Several reasons account for the disarray. First, 1987 and 1988 were years of escalating tensions and violence in the rainforest, with nearly constant empates, confrontations, and turbulence that frustrated all efforts to attain normalcy at CTA/Projeto Seringueiro, precisely when it was most critical. Internal disagreements became exacerbated in this climate. They led to Binho Marques's resignation early in 1988 when a challenger to his leadership, Reginaldo de Castelo, a doctrinaire Marxist, advocated arming the seringueiros. A few disastrous months later, Mendes fired Castelo and urged Marques to return, which he did, but only briefly, because 1988 was an intense time of great crisis; Mendes was murdered that same year.[2] Second, the constant turnover of Projeto Seringueiro staff meant virtually no continuity, stability, sustained written records, or reports to tell the story, just bits and pieces scattered here and there. Though individual staff members might have kept very complete records of their own activities, those accounts went with them when they departed CTA/Projeto Seringueiro, leaving large gaps in an already sparse institutional memory. Reinventing the wheel was a constant occupation. Third, this period was marked by the abandonment of the schools. As Marques puts it, "No one was in charge. Teachers used unfamiliar teaching materials provided by the state, everyone began teaching any way they could, and Projeto Seringueiro practically did not exist any more. . . . It was virtually dead and the CTA existed only on paper."[3]

Projeto Seringueiro Phase Two: Renewal

Chico Mendes charged Binho Marques with reviving Projeto Seringueiro and transforming it from an "ideological" project to provide literacy sufficient to run the cooperative into an "educational" project with "true" schools for the seringueiros.[4] Projeto Seringueiro's limited ideological phase was over; now its original purpose had to be joined to that of a broader educational mission to establish a network of forest schools to serve both adults and children. In Marques's first year, 1987–88, Projeto Seringueiro grew from eight to 40 schools. One might well ask how the project could begin to staff and administer the much greater number of schools when it could not keep up with the ones it already had, and when the highly charged political climate infused every action with danger. According to Marques, Mendes reasoned that if they did not expand, they would risk losing everything that the seringueiros had gained in education.[5] Mendes wanted "true" schools, but now that Projeto Seringueiro's first, or heroic, phase was over, there was no longer education for anyone; the project was dead. The expansion to 40 schools was impossible to manage, but Mendes felt there was no alternative.[6]

The only possible source of assistance was the state, but Binho Marques, like Chico Mendes, was under no illusions that the educational bureaucracy functioned at all. Fortunately, Marques had been a teacher in the public schools, where he had learned that the only way to accomplish anything was to operate through informal channels, contacts, and personal favors. He knew the rules of the game and he played it well, one reason that Mendes had hired him in the first place. Marques worked hard to develop positive relations with the personnel of the Secretariat of Education, cultivating goodwill, gaining their confidence, and convincing them of the value of Projeto Seringueiro's mission. He met frequently with officials to explain how the state could best assume its responsibilities to hire and pay teachers, and to provide lunch and teaching materials. Through close, sustained personal dealings, Marques was able to get the state to move, and to commit resources for the schools, and he himself showed them how to do it.[7]

By the time Marques left the CTA/Projeto Seringueiro in 1991, he had breathed new life into Project Rubber Tapper, stabilized it, expanded its reach, and extended its educational purpose. He had not only successfully responded to the collapse of the project, he had done so in an external climate of accelerating repression by ranchers and the local authorities in their camp. When Mendes was assassinated in December 1988, the shock waves reverberated throughout the Amazon and far beyond Brazil. However, the devastating loss was most keenly felt among the Xapuri rubber tappers, the Rural Workers Union (STR), the National Rubber Tappers Council (CNS), and the Amazonian Workers Center/Projeto Seringueiro (CTA/PS). Mendes had been the unifying, key figure, the heart and soul of the movement, and his natural leadership skills drew together individuals and groups that would never cooperate or even cross paths under normal circumstances. Without him the rubber tappers' movement was rudderless. Manoel da Cunha, a close friend of Mendes and a potential replacement, was involved in literacy work outside of Acre at the time. Mendes's cousin, Raimundo Mendes de Barros, and leading activist Marina Silva, who later became minister of the environment for the Amazon under Inácio "Lula" da Silva, ultimately emerged as Mendes's successors; however, in the immediate aftermath of the assassination, there was only shock and grief. Mendes had received death threats for years, and very specific ones for the previous month that he had reported to the police; still, the extractivists were caught off-guard when the inevitable occurred.

Binho Marques was personally devastated. Further, he disagreed sharply with the direction that some members of the seringueiros' movement wished to take after Mendes's death; he also was disaffected by the inability of the National Rubber Tappers Council (CNS) to come up with sound projects for the funds that began to pour in from the outside. Marques recalls:

> Sources of financing appeared from all over to support projects in the rainforest, but the movement itself did not have its own project; rather, the leaders made their project according to the resources that came in. . . . I disagreed with the coordinators of the National Rubber Tappers Council (CNS) at that time. Things were not going well at all; I was miserable, and we suffered without Chico's leadership. . . . I didn't have any support from the CNS leadership. Actually I didn't have the support of anyone.[8]

Marques's bitter disappointment lasted for several years, until Jorge Viana, for whom Marques had campaigned, was elected mayor of Rio Branco in 1994. The timing was right for Marques to accept Viana's offer to become municipal secretary of education for that city's first ever progressive administration.

Projeto Seringueiro Phase Three:
Extractive Reserves

Meanwhile, in 1989 Djalcir "Pingo" Ferreira, already well known for his brilliance in teacher training and curriculum development, entered CTA/ Projeto Seringueiro, having been asked the year before by Binho Marques and Jorge Viana to work with a new team on developing an educational plan for the extractive reserves. When he came on board, he immediately reinforced Freire's dialogical method, reasserted the environmental base of Projeto Seringueiro, and stressed its crucial teacher accompaniment component, a uniquely distinguishing feature of Projeto Seringueiro, which, as previously noted, involved ongoing encouragement of teachers.[9] Jorge Viana and Binho Marques's invitation to Pingo Ferreira provides another example of the ever-expanding ripples from Projeto Seringueiro's unlikely pebble. Manoel da Cunha, when he returned to Acre in 1992, worked on the plan with Ferreira and his team, which included Francisca "Chiquinha" da Silva, whose interview follows. Their charge was to come up with a workable plan and materials for students and their teachers in the new extractive reserve schools. They were to focus on teaching comprehension of math concepts, the four basic operations, and on reading a very brief text—still an enormous task in the rainforest's oral culture, especially in the more remote reserves. The mission of the CTA/Projeto Seringueiro educational team was to prepare students and teachers to "understand both their own world and that outside the forest."[10]

The key actors in the evolution of Projeto Seringueiro were now in place:

1. Binho Marques, who rekindled the extinguished Projeto Seringueiro flame at Chico Mendes's behest and who later as secretary of education and then as governor worked consistently to make his motto "education for all" a reality.

2. Pingo Ferreira, who insisted on excellence in teacher training, accompaniment, and curriculum development.
3. Manoel da Cunha, one of the four original Projeto Seringueiro teachers in 1981, who later designed curriculum and
workshops with Ferreira, and then moved on to begin indigenous education in Acre.

Though they are colleagues and friends, these unusually talented individuals did not always agree. Binho Marques, for example, wanted to
cast a wider if imperfect educational net, while Pingo Ferreira was unwilling to sacrifice quality for quantity, and Manoel da Cunha was a
trailblazing pioneer, always seeking new challenges. But they all agreed
on the common goal of bringing education to unserved populations. In
the 1990s this meant focusing on the reserves.

However, plans for education, as well as for chronically neglected
health programs, got off to a rocky start in the reserves because implementation procedures were nonexistent and the financial assistance
promised by the state was sporadic, largely because of the haste with
which everything was carried out.[11] Viana, who became governor in
1999, was eager to start schools in the reserves, which meant careful co-
ordination went by the board. Even so, Pingo Ferreira and Manoel da
Cunha continued to work during the 1990s, with and without assistance, to plan and conduct teacher training and systematize requirements
for teachers.

Ferreira directed the remarkably effective teacher training seminars,
which took place yearly through 2005, until every last cent for training
and accompaniment had been squeezed from meager budgets. Ferreira
and da Cunha together wrote, or supervised the writing of, most of the
pedagogical materials used from the 1990s until the final teachers workshop. During the 1990s, Project Rubber Tapper's education team brought
in technical experts to advise in areas like reforestation and seed management, and educational consultants like Maria Lúcia Martins to co-
conduct workshops for teachers. Martins and Ferreira collaborated on a
pedagogical text, *A Lição da Samaúma* (The Lesson of the Samaúma
Tree), based on their workshop experiences in which contributions from
teachers had inspired the educational team to revise Projeto Seringueiro's

math program. Thus it was that from the decree establishing the extractive reserves in 1988 through 2005, CTA/Projeto Seringueiro provided teacher training in the reserves.

The CTA, FUNTAC (Fundação Tecnológica do Acre [Technological Foundation of Acre]), and the then secretary of education for Acre (SEC/AC, now the SEE) had entered into an agreement in 1990, renewed every two years afterward, establishing the bases for collaborative work in the extractive reserves and neighboring seringais where the project was already active, as well as in the state forest of Antimari. The then SEC had as its responsibility to provide the CTA/Projeto Seringueiro with educational professionals from the public network to compose the technical team of the project, to offer provisional 10-month contracts for teachers, and to provide educational supplies and lunch service for the schools. CTA/Projeto Seringueiro's job was to train these teachers and produce didactic materials appropriate to the sociocultural context of the seringais.[12] By 1991 much-needed norms had been established for opening and closing schools, and also regarding requirements for becoming a teacher, with specific competencies listed, and cultural content outlined, along with a description of the responsibilities of teacher, student, family, educational team, consultants, and the role of regular planning and evaluation. From 1991 on, the reserve schools gradually acquired definite shape and structure.

In all of this, the most important aspect, and one that Pingo Ferreira consistently stressed, was the basic Freireian philosophy of building upon what the student already knows, the student's "intellectual universe"— in this case, the local forest culture and experiences.[13] With Ferreira, da Cunha, and the educational team's new structure in place, the unchecked growth of schools stopped; their numbers dropped from 30 in 1991 to a more manageable 27 in 1999, with approximately four more schools established in extractive reserves between 2000 and 2008.[14]

Teaching workshops were held wherever people could attend—at various forest sites, the least expensive locale, as well as in Xapuri and Rio Branco. The problem was always cost and lack of infrastructure, which made ongoing accompaniment and follow-up of teachers precarious, but a fiercely committed core team including Pingo Ferreira, Manoel da Cunha, and Ademir Pereira, whose interview follows, persisted. From the very first workshop in 1983, even before the reserves were established, teacher training had been central to the success of Projeto Seringueiro schools. Ferreira describes it this way:

> I can't overemphasize the importance of the workshops. The teachers absolutely loved them and looked forward to them with eager anticipation because they were a time of learning, sharing, and socializing. Teachers would go to great lengths to attend. To give you an idea of their dedication, we have one teacher who traveled seven hours on foot just to arrive at the road in Xapuri where she could get a ride to the workshop. With her first paycheck she purchased a pressure cooker to make meal preparation easier for her family while she was away. With her second one, she bought a horse to facilitate travel from the forest to Xapuri.[15]

Ferreira explains that it is difficult for people in the city to realize how different everything is in the forest, given the vast distances between communities and the difficulty of travel. This makes for a very distinct culture from that of the city, and one in which extended workshops are a necessity. Ferreira also reminds urban dwellers of the following:

> Our teachers are all barely literate in the beginning. Everything is new to them, and they have to build skills and self-confidence at the same time. The team, the teacher trainers, have to be very sensitive to that fact. . . . That's why we have to have training and have it according to their time frame. But what MEC [Ministry of Education] does is leave the book with the teacher, provide no training, and say "Here, use this."[16]

Ferreira recounts the difficulty of retraining teachers for the reserves, most of whom, even if they themselves were from rural areas, had previously had access only to standardized texts from the MEC in Brasília which tended to "massify" and "homogenize." To Ferreira, such centralized texts, written by urban bureaucrats, funnel all learning into abstract written molds, whereas forest culture is concrete and oral, hence the need for methodological adjustments in training teachers. For one thing, Ferreira taught the new reserve teachers how to teach in a multidisciplinary fashion—for example, not separating Portuguese and math from economics, biology, or psychology, as in graded schools. These, he knew, should be taught together as part of problem-posing projects, such as how to reduce disease by filtering drinking water, how to improve quality of agricultural products and increase income from the cooperative, how best to maintain the school premises, or how to address the issue of domestic violence.[17] In order to accomplish these objectives, the Projeto Seringueiro team dedicated significant blocks of time, not only to teacher workshops, but also to the highly regarded accompaniment that followed, spending weeks and even months visiting and supporting teachers and communities even in the most isolated areas.

Ferreira used booklets produced by the educational team and teachers during teacher workshops to teach names of flora and fauna—the types of animals that inhabit the rivers, ravines, and shallows—in order to help the teachers themselves learn and then, later, teach their own students how to classify scientifically types of soil, water, trees, and animals and to utilize reference materials. After teachers have accomplished these tasks in workshops and accompaniment, then they learn about the polar bear from the Ministry of Education book. By then, teachers can go to the map, find the polar bear's habitat, classify it the same way they did local animals, and use its scientific name. This is linking the particular with the universal.[18] Ferreira comments on the cultural significance of this approach:

> When the teacher does his work well, he does not limit himself to the local, but he begins with the local and places it in the larger world. If the teacher just sticks to the polar bear, the giraffe, the animals that they have on TV and in the circus, the students talk only about the animals that we do not have in Brazil. That type of approach makes the student feel that his surroundings are somehow inferior, so our approach is to say, "Look, here in the forest science exists." Culturally, it is a necessity to link the individual to the place where he lives. If he becomes dislocated, he doesn't understand or appreciate his locale. . . . In the forest, people know a great deal, but what they know is not valued by the outside world, including the producers of educational materials [like MEC], and the seringueiros, in turn, devalue their own culture. It is basic Freireian philosophy to value and build upon what the learner already knows, his local culture and experiences. That is why the little booklets on animals and fish that the teachers produced

in the workshops are so important. When they see their own stories in their own language, together with the classification of the animals, such as vertebrates, invertebrates, mammals, they feel highly valued, they have made a book, which is amazing to them.[19]

Slowly but surely, Projeto Seringueiro's *Poronga* began to illuminate the forest once more, as it had done when Mary Allegretti held the very first class in Seringal Nazaré that stormy night in 1981. Results in the reserves have been surprisingly good, according to Ferreira, who does not bestow praise lightly. It is surprising considering the haste with which Viana's government desired to accomplish everything, the parlous state of financing, and the daunting challenges of distance, communication, transportation, and construction presented by the rainforest itself. For its success in extending basic education to forest populations, CTA/Projeto Seringueiro was awarded the prestigious Itaú/UNICEF Prize in 1993, 1995, and 1997.

Education for All/*Educação para Todos*

When Binho Marques became secretary of education for Acre (1999–2007) under then governor Jorge Viana, one of his first objectives was to extend Projeto Seringueiro's accomplishments to all rural schools in the state, not just those in the reserves. He had visited Colombia in 1996 on an educational mission when he was municipal secretary of education; there he became acquainted with the work of Escolativa, a rural education program, and brought back materials for the CTA/Projeto Seringueiro Educational Team to study. His intention was to incorporate some of Escolativa's features, including its ideas for going beyond the first four years of basic education through *ensino médio*, roughly grades four through eight. What Marques most wanted, however, was to see all rural schools adopt Projeto Seringueiro's methodology, teacher training, and accompaniment models. CTA/Projeto Seringueiro, however, declined Marques's invitation, partly because of internal divisions among staff members, but primarily because of Pingo Ferreira's concern that quality would be sacrificed by enlarging the scale. He doubted that Projeto Seringueiro's staff would be able to sustain Projeto Seringueiro's hallmarks of extensive training and accompaniment of teachers.[20] Marques was disappointed because "the one who has been excellent in Projeto Seringueiro is Pingo [Ferreira]; whatever he does is outstanding, and I very much needed his expertise on my team."[21] Manoel da Cunha disagreed with Ferreira's decision, and left CTA/Projeto Seringueiro in 1999 in order to work for the government.

In 2000 Marques, as secretary of education for Acre, appointed da Cunha director of the newly created Indigenous Education office for the state of Acre, a position in which da Cunha applied the Project Rubber Tapper model, this time not to *caboclo* riverine communities, or to extractive reserves, but to indigenous populations, in yet another example of the influence of Projeto Seringueiro's methodology and mission. As da Cunha observes, "In Indigenous Education, I carry out projects based on my work with Projeto Seringueiro, which has been an ongoing influence."[22] Projeto Seringueiro's nongraded, interdisciplinary model with its academic year adapted to the work rhythm of the forest has been essential in indigenous education in Acre, as has the fact that students and teachers create almost all their materials together. Da Cunha remarks, "This is exactly what we did in Projeto Seringueiro when students produced their own books. That's when school becomes a living thing."[23] Prior to 2000 there had been in Acre absolutely no state effort in indigenous education at all. It had been left to a few NGOs, such as the Pro-Indian Commission (CPI), linked to the Catholic Church and missionary groups.

Meanwhile, with ever-shrinking staff and funds due to the brain drain from NGOs like the CTA/Projeto Seringueiro to the now progressive city and state government, and unable to care properly for its 40 schools, CTA/Projeto Seringueiro was forced by circumstances in 1999 to turn over to the state the operation of 32 of its 40 schools. Viana's new state government, unlike previous ones, completely shared the project's educational and social philosophy. After all, Governor Viana, Secretary of Education Marques, and soon-to-be-named Director of Indigenous Education da Cunha had all previously served for years as teachers, education team members, or directors of CTA/Projeto Seringueiro. This was definitely a new situation for the NGO, accustomed to being a pressure group on the outs with the government; now, they *were* the government. The result was not just a brain drain from the civil to the state sector, but also a confusion regarding the identity and role of NGOs in the new circumstance. At Pingo Ferreira's insistence, the project retained control of eight schools, the "best eight," as Marques ruefully remarks. For his part, Ferreira continued to strive for excellence in teacher training, curriculum development, and accompaniment not only for those eight schools, but also for all those set up in the reserves.

At the same time, in an effort to standardize and improve the quality of teaching throughout Brazil, the federal government in 1999 had created the Pro-formation (Pro-formação) program, which required lay, or uncertified, teachers to complete certain course requirements for certification. In Acre, teachers in rural and forest schools who had been granted provisional contracts with very low salary were among the uncertified rural teachers in the state. Though statistics are unavailable, when one considers that even as late as 2000 there were very few schools in rural areas, and that the Amazon region is the most rural in all Brazil, one can appreciate that the net cast by Pro-formation drew in most rural teachers in the state. Projeto Seringueiro teachers, nearly all of whom were both uncertified and unschooled, at least formally, also participated in the federally mandated Pro-formation program. Projeto Seringueiro teachers, though uncertified and unschooled, were not untrained, and they received the highest ratings of all participants in all aspects of Pro-formation. They particularly excelled in problem-solving assignments and were praised by program instructors for their disciplined work habits. Most other teachers had not developed the critical sense or discipline necessary to perform well on Pro-formation's significant problem-solving component, or to complete the large amount of homework required in the intensive 45-day program.[24] It is no coincidence that from his very first day at CTA/Projeto Seringueiro in 1989, Ferreira had insisted upon critical, problem-posing training and disciplined work habits for teachers. His insistence paid off.

Taking teacher training for rural instructors a giant step further, the state government in 2007, under Marques's leadership as secretary of education, sponsored a program to extend the education of rural teachers to the university level. Nearly all 40 Projeto Seringueiro instructors, most of them former rubber tappers—Projeto Seringueiro students who had acquired their own literacy through Projeto Seringueiro's schools—immediately took advantage of this opportunity, concentrating in areas such as pedagogy, math, geography, history, and biology. Binho Marques thus moved closer to achieving his goal of education for all.

Projeto Seringueiro: Influence and Legacy

The influence of Projeto Seringueiro through upward mobility for former teachers and students is clear in this trajectory. Education has opened up opportunities for individuals that no one would have even dreamed possible before the advent of Projeto Seringueiro. At the same time, in areas where Projeto Seringueiro has been strong, more seringueiros are remaining in the seringal, for very few today are moving to the city; this is due in large measure to the environmental basis of their education, which has enabled them, so far, to live sustainably in the forest. Seringueiros, having internalized the empowering message of Project Rubber Tapper, have developed a more critical worldview, and they have come to value themselves, their forest culture, and the importance of their work, especially as they are daily witnesses to the ravages of deforestation. They defend the forest by staying and keeping it standing. Rubber is no longer the sole mainstay of the forest economy, but thanks in large measure to the project, seringueiros are learning new ways to live from the forest again. They remain not because they have a school there but because the schools have helped them establish viable economic activities and given them the knowledge of how to make the activities work, as in seed management, reforestation, and small agricultural projects offered in some reserve schools. As da Cunha explains, "This is important schoolwork because one who is involved in a productive project does not migrate out of his community."[25]

In cataloging the project's influences, mention must be made of Projeto Seringueiro's bold example of addressing gender issues and modeling gender equity for teachers and the communities they represent. Though it has been very slow, as we shall see in the following interviews, this practice has amounted to a quiet revolution, especially when one remembers that 100 years ago the seringueiro who produced a large quantity of rubber could purchase a wife. Projeto Seringueiro never had a gendered division of labor and consistently worked hard to demonstrate equality.[26]

Additionally, da Cunha has commented that the influence of the project on indigenists has been considerable, pointing out that the Pro-Indian Commission (CPI) first used Projeto Seringueiro's *Poronga* very early on without any change at all. Since Indians had been the original seringueiros, that text seemed to work culturally, but that, like the subject of gender, is another story.[27]

Clearly, CTA/Projeto Seringueiro developed a special competency in extractive education, with additional social, political, and economic benefits radiating out to the larger community. However, as da Cunha points out, as time went on, it became clear that neither the CTA/Projeto Seringueiro nor the government knew how to communicate effectively with each other, so they did not move forward together as well as they could have. The CTA umbrella was an NGO in search of its mission from the 1990s, when the government began to assume many of its functions and even bought expensive educational services from the Fundação Roberto Marino associated with TV/Globo instead of making use of the CTA/Projeto Seringueiro's local talent pool, a questionable use of precious funds.[28]

On the other hand, the government was ahead of the curve on indigenous education, which all previous governments had neglected. By 2007 da Cunha could point to the 74 indigenous teachers in the interior prepared to teach through middle school, and to the 52 more who were ready to go, thanks to state support and the Projeto Seringueiro model. These are impressive numbers. Further, as was the case with Projeto Seringueiro teachers, indigenous teachers are moving to specially designed university teacher preparation courses, thanks to da Cunha and his Projeto Seringueiro experience.[29]

Like the Department of Indigenous Education, the Department of Rural Education in which it is housed is itself creating many points of light from the Projeto Seringueiro lantern, as we shall see in interviews with Francisca Chiquinha da Silva, who wrote a master's thesis on Projeto Seringueiro, and Ivanilde Lopes da Silva, former base community monitor, rural teacher, and early organizer of the social movement.

Thus we see that Projeto Seringueiro evolved from a small courageous effort with immediate political goals to a larger disorganized program, to moribund status, to rebirth, to extension to the reserves, to gradual absorption by the state, which brought with it the kinds of identity and mission issues that many NGOs face today. The problems of success or absorption include an unwieldy and unwilling bureaucracy, and bureaucrats who may know or care nothing about education, as Chiquinha da Silva points out in her interview. Projeto Seringueiro's embattled existence, internal divisions, and paucity of resources caused the flame to sputter and go out for a while, but it was rekindled thanks to a critical mass of creative, flexible, and dedicated educational teams, administrators, and teachers, led in the leanest of times by Binho Marques, Pingo Ferreira, and Manoel da Cunha.

Projeto Seringueiro is one example of Acre's successful social movement of the 1980s in which nearly every segment of civil society, urban and rural, from teachers to domestic workers, and above all to rubber tappers, mobilized to protest the military government and the destruction of the rainforest, and to demand a new democratic government for the state. In that process, NGOs and alternative organizations like Projeto Seringueiro illustrate the power of social mobilization in effecting change, in this case, in educational and environmental policy. The project's educational and social contributions reverberate far beyond the palm-thatched shelters that served as the first tentative schools.

Acre's debt to Projeto Seringueiro's consciousness-raising experiment was officially recognized by Governor Marques in October 2008 in Xapuri with festivities, a theatrical presentation, exhibits of Projeto Seringueiro photos and books—including the original *Poronga*—emotional speeches, and fond reflections by participants. The commemoration of the project's 26-year existence was part of the effort by the Marina Silva Biblioteca da Floresta and the CTA to collect the dispersed pieces of Projeto Seringueiro's history and eventually make them accessible to everyone.

At the ceremony, one of the first local monitors, Leide Aquino, who in the beginning gave classes to unlettered seringueiros with only a chalkboard suspended from a mango tree, was asked to describe what Projeto Seringueiro meant to her: "For me, Projeto Seringueiro signified both struggle and victory. From my point of view, Projeto Seringueiro and the winning of the reserves are the greatest things we have ever achieved in our municipality; they began everything and opened up the possibilities for people like myself to advance."[30] Others pointed out that now that the state administers the schools and has added more levels in locales like Xapuri, seringueiros can continue their education beyond the first four years, completing eight years without having to leave the forest. Finally, Ademir Pereira, one of the first teachers to respond to Mary Allegretti and Chico Mendes's bold vision in 1981, expressed his gratification that Projeto Seringueiro had accomplished its mission, for now nearly all adults in Xapuri can read and write at least some. However, for him, Projeto Seringueiro still lives on: "I would not say that Projeto Seringueiro is over; for there are still other roads we need to travel, offering support and encouragement in the area of education."[31] Finally, all those present at the commemoration acknowledged Projeto Seringueiro's Freireian base as crucial to the success of the project:

> Poronga was based on the teachings of Paulo Freire and adapted to the reality of the forest dweller. We did not begin with words like dollar, airplane, telephone; no, we began with paca, tatu, samaúma, and all that was familiar to the seringueiros. From that base of study, cooperatives were formed, communication among seringueiros evolved, and they began to administer their own finances, understand their rights and duties as extractivist workers.[32]

As NGOs, such as the CTA, grapple with the need to reinvent themselves, and as they question their relevance in a society in which the state government has rejected both military and neoliberal dictates in order to reassume its traditional civic responsibilities, it is well to remember that NGOs always have a vital role to play in public life. That role changes, of course, but even the most democratic government benefits from a critical voice, external pressure, and an alternative vision—not to mention that the government cannot do it all. For example, for every hard-fought protection for the forest and its populations, another threat crops up, most recently the alarming increase in deforestation brought about by the extensive cultivation of sugar cane for ethanol fuel, of which Brazil is now the world's largest exporter. The main concern with deforestation currently is among small-scale producers, including those in the extractive reserves. The rising tide of global economic interests does not lift all boats or even all yachts; rather, it threatens to dash local cultures

ɔmies on the rocks of unsustainable export-led development
ecked greed. Thus, NGOs and a highly conscientisized, in-
ɔblic are just as essential now as when Chico Mendes first began
organizing seringueiros in the 1970s. Thanks to the Rural Workers
Union (STR), the cooperatives, the Workers Party (PT), the National
Rubber Tappers Council (CNS), the extractive reserves, and CTA/Projeto
Seringueiro, the concept of environmental defense is now deeply embed-
ded in the curriculum, consciousness, and worldview of the populace.

Projeto Seringueiro was in some ways a victim of its own success. As
progressive governments replaced the development-obsessed dictatorship, the hard work of Mendes, the Union, the base communities, and
the broader social movement ushered in radical changes in government
as well as in attitudes toward education. The unusually rich vein of gifted
leaders at CTA/Projeto Seringueiro began to be mined in 1991 to serve
the new progressive government. Jorge Viana, Binho Marques, Manoel
da Cunha, Chiquinha da Silva, and finally, Pingo Ferreira, the last hold-
out, gradually moved from the civil to the government sector, where they
were able to put the resources of the state behind their ideas. They left
an NGO vacuum to be sure, but they carried the project's mission with
them until it became part of the state system, something Governor Marques had been hoping to achieve since 1991. Thus we see that Projeto
Seringueiro worked itself out of a job as it graduated into the larger system. One might say that Projeto Seringueiro accomplished for education
what liberation theology accomplished for religion, only on a much smaller
scale. They each came in with an urgent social and political mission, were
persecuted by authorities, made serious mistakes, achieved dramatic vic-
tories, profoundly altered the lives and worldviews of thousands of people,
and changed institutions. They each left valuable legacies: a heightened
critical consciousness, a community and environmental ethic, expanded
citizen participation in the political process, and proof of the importance
of becoming active subjects rather than passive objects in the historical
process. These are no small accomplishments. Currently, this is a time
both of anxiety and hope for NGOs in Acre as the civil sector seeks to re-
define itself.

In Part II of this study, we see the effect that Projeto Seringueiro has
had on individual lives, and observe up close just what education for personal and popular empowerment has meant in the seringais of Xapuri.

Notes

1. Interviews with Arnóbio "Binho" Marques Júnior. Interviews by author. May 22, 2006; October 8, 2008. Rio Branco, Acre.
2. Ibid.
3. Ibid.
4. Ibid.
5. Ibid.
6. Ibid.
7. Ibid.
8. Ibid.
9. Interviews with Djalcir "Pingo" Ferreira. Interviews by author. May 25 and 26, 2006; August 8, 9, and 10, 2007; October 5 and 6, 2008. Rio Branco, Acre.
10. Interviews with Manoel Estébio Cavalcante da Cunha. Interviews by author. May 22, 2006; August 5, 2007; October 10, 2008. Rio Branco, Acre.
11. Ibid.
12. CTA/Projeto Seringueiro, *Proposta Político Pedagógica: um Projeto com Características Únicas para as Escolas da Floresta 2000,* Photocopy, 41.
13. Ibid., 49–52.
14. Ibid., 42.
15. Interviews with Ferreira.
16. Ibid.
17. *Proposta Política,* 28.
18. Interviews with Ferreira.
19. Ibid.
20. Interviews with da Cunha.
21. Interviews with Marques.
22. Interviews with da Cunha.
23. Ibid.
24. Ibid.
25. Ibid.
26. Ibid.
27. Ibid.
28. Ibid.
29. Ibid.
30. Elynalia Lima, "Projeto seringueiro: 25 anos de ensino pioneiro na Floresta," October 25, 2008, http://www.ac.gov.br/bibliotecadafloresta/biblioteca.
31. Ibid.
32. Ibid.

Photo by Djalcir "Pingo" Ferreira.

Seringueiro's House, Seringal São Francisco do Espalha, Xapuri.

Photo by Djalcir "Pingo" Ferreira.

Going to School, Igarapé Jacu, Upper Rio Xapuri.

Photo by Djalcir "Pingo" Ferreira.

Vitória School, Seringal Cachoeira.

Photo by Djalcir "Pingo" Ferreira.

São Francisco School, Macauã National Forest.

Photo by Djalcir "Pingo" Ferreira.

Classroom Activity, Ivair Higino School,
Chico Mendes Extractive Reserve.

Photo by Djalcir "Pingo" Ferreira.

Open-Air Class, Nova Esperança School II, Riozinho, Rio Xapuri.

Part II

Voices

4

Points of Light

Introduction

The voices in this chapter are those of the earliest Projeto Seringueiro teachers in Xapuri who, since the 1970s, have served as points of light guiding their communities. The first, Ademir Pereira, recalls Project Rubber Tapper's origins and former students who have since become community leaders. He also contrasts Projeto Seringueiro's past accomplishments with contemporary hardships, namely the administrative and financial shortcomings of the umbrella CTA. Ademir Pereira's devotion to the students and teachers he has served for over 25 years stands out in his straightforward, candid account.

Dercy Teles, the second voice of this chapter, was one of the original team of four Projeto Seringueiro teachers and is today one of Xapuri's most respected leaders. She currently serves as a community health worker in her native seringal, and as president of Xapuri's Rural Workers Union (STRX). Her account places Project Rubber Tapper in the context of the base communities and the union, and offers a sharp rejection of recent local politics as well as national environmental practices, particularly the extensive cultivation of sugar cane for biofuel production. Her strong ethical sense and independent spirit have given Dercy Teles the courage to speak truth to power on many occasions.

Antonia Pereira, the third voice, shares the environmental concerns of Dercy Teles, as she remembers her many years of service with Projeto Seringueiro, the base communities, the union, and more recently, her work as a preschool teacher for the state. Antonia Pereira's account highlights the intimate relationship between the base communities, the union, and the school, and calls for a renewed defense of the forest by the people of Xapuri.

Though they differ in personality and interests, these three long-standing community leaders have a great deal in common. All either live or have lived in the forest; all are natives of Xapuri; all have received some combination of formal and informal education; none was trained to be a teacher or had any intention of becoming a teacher; all were deeply influenced by Chico Mendes, whom they knew personally and with whom they worked; all signed on to Projeto Seringueiro because they wanted to achieve social and environmental justice for the seringueiro. Finally, all three voices speak from personal experience to the theme of popular empowerment through education, as we shall soon discover.

Ademir Pereira Rodrigues

It was 1981, and I was working with a friend on his house, when I looked up to see Chico Mendes and Mary Allegretti standing there. They

Photo by author.

Ademir Pereira Rodrigues

had come to invite everyone in the community to a meeting about a school for seringueiros. I attended and heard Chico give a wonderful, inspiring speech about an opportunity that no one had ever discussed before. Previously, you would have local officials come out every now and then and promise to do things for us, and, of course, they never delivered. But no one had ever promised anything to communities far from the city, where you have to arrive by boat or on foot, and no politician would enter such locales in the first place. That's why I say that having a meeting about a school for our community was unheard of. Chico and Mary had already held meetings in two other places; we were the third. They had already chosen one of the teachers, Pedro Teles, who could barely sign his name, but who was a good person and willing to teach and learn.

In the conversations during the meeting, everyone agreed that the school's objective was to end the economic control of the seringalistas who stole from the seringueiros twice: first, by making tappers buy sup-plies only from them, and sell their rubber only to them; and second, by cheating the tappers in the price paid for their rubber. The seringalista could record any weight and price that he wished and talk about the weather at the same time, because the seringueiro couldn't read or do math. In 1981, after the meeting, I helped build the first school, with a packed-earth floor, a palm roof, and classes began in 1982.

I had been fortunate enough to finish elementary school, which was more than Pedro, my teacher and friend, and he asked me to be his as-sistant. I was single at the time and didn't mind teaching on weekends, which is when we held classes. I worked happily for no pay for several years, no problem. I had gone to school in Xapuri and briefly in Rio Branco. I had lived first in Xapuri, then in the seringal, then back in Xapuri again. I received a contract shortly after the CTA was created, and they negotiated the teachers' pay with the secretary of education, but it was several years before I actually began receiving a salary. Teach-ing was producing good results, and the number of students kept grow-ing. In those early years, my school alone produced three health agents, two teachers, several cooperative agents, and other community leaders.

Then things started moving way too fast, and in the mid-1980s we jumped up to 40 schools, which was just impossible. Projeto Seringueiro didn't grow, it overflowed. It was a disaster because we had no way of ac-companying, supporting, all these new teachers. I decided to leave in 1989 after Chico's death, but first I trained people to take my place be-cause you have to do things responsibly.

Right away, however, the Projeto Seringueiro coordinating team asked me to reconsider, saying they needed me. So I stayed on, this time as an advisor and teacher of teachers, which has been a major part of my life ever since. Some schools are very difficult to reach, but I visit them with great joy and I keep going back, because I love the people and the work. Lately, the situation is not favorable, financially speaking, since I have no money. If you were to ask me what is the situation of the Proj-eto now [2006], I would have to answer there is no Projeto. I hear tell there's a Projeto, but there's nothing.

However, there have been so many positive moments. The greatest thing is actually being there in the community. What a different reception

I receive now from when I first started visiting the seringais. At the beginning, people would say, "Good afternoon," then they would be very quiet; it was extremely difficult to converse. Part of the problem was that we were strangers, but a big part was also that they didn't feel they were capable of keeping up with the social rhythm of others, the outside world. The seringueiros thought of themselves as inferior to other people, and they would hang back. You still see that in some places. But today I go to these communities, and the animation I see! Everyone wants to talk at the same time; the child comes up and shows me the work he has done; the father and the mother talk, question, debate; the community has changed greatly. It was not radical, all at once, no, it was drop by drop. And some of those communities, when I first visited, the child had no idea how to hold a pencil, but today he is a teacher, a health or cooperative agent, or president of the union. That is the reward. It makes me very happy indeed.

Even though I had lived in the seringal myself, I still had to learn over the years how to deal with the forest people. You have to be very cautious because of their traditions and customs. You can't just barge in there and go about changing everything; you have to be very respectful. Of course, you do interfere in their culture, but you have to do just a little bit here and a little bit there, very slowly. I've been making visits for over 20 years now, and it's wonderful to see the positive changes taking place in the seringueiros themselves and in their communities.

That's why it is very frustrating to see the great need, but have no staff to meet it. Every day people ask me to go out to the seringal and help the teachers because they need accompaniment, but where is the team? I'm the team, but I no longer have funds for anything. What's up with the CTA in Rio Branco? There's no help for us here in Xapuri. The problem is the turnover in leadership in the CTA in recent years; people keep coming and going, and no one knows where the reports and files are that I sent them. It's very disorganized!

There's quite a difference between then and now, because I look back and remember beautiful things. Take the *Mala de Leitura* [Suitcase of Readings], for example, in children's literature, both classical and Brazilian. Cila Pereira da Silva did a great job on that, and later Socorro D'Avila de Oliveira did, too. It would've been even better if we had had more follow-through, but staff members were coming and going, and then Pingo Ferreira and I took it over; he loves the seringal and the seringueiros like I do. The *Mala* was hugely successful in bringing literature into the forest; it was a new concept for an oral culture, as was the idea that you could read for pleasure.

I have many facts in my head, and I can tell you that more than 2,000 students have passed through these schools. Some go to Xapuri, but just a few, I'd say about 200 over the years, perhaps fewer. The great majority are staying in the seringal. This is another accomplishment of Projeto Seringueiro. I'd say between 99% and 100% of the teachers in Projeto Seringueiro schools were first students in the schools; they became literate in order to be able to teach. Between 80 and 100 people have become teachers.

The hard part is to take a teacher from here, the town of Xapuri, and send them to the seringal to teach. Even though Xapuri is very small, it is still a different world from the seringal. The teachers usually don't last a year; if they do, it's because they don't want to lose their salary. They usually are not interested in developing long-term projects with the communities; they just want to leave. Often, they have a disagreement with someone in the community because they are unhappy there and they don't understand the local culture. It is very difficult to adjust to living in the seringal, so they leave and the community is upset, making things tougher for the next teacher. That's why the Projeto tries hard to hire teachers from the community itself. We have criteria we use in selecting people to become teachers. They must: (1) have no vices, (2) be well regarded by the community, (3) have an affinity for the community, and (4) be able to read and write very brief texts. At first our criterion was that teachers only be able to sign their names. We have made much progress in bringing writing into an oral culture, but it takes time. That's why the training courses and the accompaniment have been so crucial.

Within a 30-day intensive training course, teachers learn an amazing amount, and then they go back and begin teaching. Here's where the accompaniment is so important because they need that follow-up. To visit some teachers I must travel 20 hours on foot from Xapuri to their home, then two more hours to get to the school. Generally, the lower the level of the teacher, the more time I spend accompanying him or her.

Projeto Seringueiro has changed the way of thinking of the seringueiros. They learn first about their own geography and environment;
they discover their own world. Then they broaden their horizons. For example, a teacher in one of the workshops discovered something very interesting. He learned about the world outside through geography by
tracing the course of the Xapuri River on a map. Before, he had never
seen a map, nor had he been outside of Xapuri's environs. As far as he
knew, the river began and ended in Xapuri. Then he saw that it emptied
into another, which emptied into the Amazon, and finally, the ocean.
He saw from the map that the river is part of something larger, and he
learned that he, too, is connected to a larger world.

I am from a humble family from the Northeast. My mother was the
daughter of a Paraense and an Indian. There were 10 children, so I knew
that I had to support myself as an adolescent. I had been doing various
jobs for a while around my native Xapuri, when Chico and Mary came
to announce the Projeto Seringueiro meeting. I am so thankful that I
attended, because it changed my entire life and gave me a purpose. Before I retire, I would really like to see my work continued because soon
I will no longer have legs that can climb up and down those steep riverbanks in the seringais. When that time comes, I would like to pass my
work on, and I would also like to have a modest pension to live on. I finished the university yesterday and presented my project. It went well,
and they gave me the highest grade and said it was the best work of all
85 students. That was very gratifying, and I am very grateful to Pingo
Ferreira and to Graciete Zaire, who was a consultant to CTA/Projeto
Seringueiro. They both encouraged me and helped me financially, because even though the course is free, you still have to pay fees.

The relationship between the CTA and the state has its pluses and
minuses. The state has actually been very responsible, unlike the CTA.
The secretary of education pays the teachers, provides teaching materials, some of which we use, and the school lunch. What I can't tell is what
the CTA is contributing to Projeto Seringueiro at this time, what their
objective is; they seem to have no direction or resources.

If the CTA were to work with the government on the Escolativa rural
education project, that would be great, but it has to be done carefully.
You can't go into an area where the community is not already organized.

But where you have organization and key community members who have been there for some time, and who have a critical vision of our municipality, then you can enter because the community is prepared. You have to have local leaders and communities with a school experience, where they are used to working in groups to build things, like the school.

There are other communities that have not had good experiences with groups from the outside coming in. For example, people go in there and run roughshod over local customs; they bring all the materials in and pay the locals to help with meetings, arrangements, construction, everything. Now those communities won't do anything without being paid; they don't want to work for nothing. There was even a time when the CTA itself did this, paid people for community work, the exact opposite of *mutirão* (volunteer work groups) and community cooperation in the building of a school, for example. It happened when the CTA had lots of money and projects at their disposal. They carried out projects and spent money like it was one big party, but they didn't have the slightest idea what they were doing or what the consequences would be. Those responsible are long gone, perhaps to some other unfortunate community. But they left a bad feeling in some communities that is still difficult for us to overcome. The experience those communities had was that the CTA came, messed things up, and left.

Our direct relationship with the secretary of education is very good, because of Binho Marques [Marques had not yet become governor]. It's easy to work with him since he used to be president of the CTA and knew how to administer the organization properly. He knows the complete history of our area, he was a Projeto Seringueiro teacher, and he used to do what I do today. Jorge Viana, the governor, he, too, was formerly an excellent president of the CTA, and he came and visited me also. Our relationship with the government has been very good. Chiquinha da Silva is also a wonderful person. She is the head of the Department of Education for the rural zone.

The state is not the problem; it's the CTA. For past three years, the CTA hasn't had any resources for anything. In fact, many times during the past three years I have had to pay in order to carry out my work, but now I can no longer afford to do that. I used to put my *moto* [motorbike] in my small boat, take the river as far as I could, and then go by moto into the interior, and finally walk when there was no path. Now, however, my salary of 400 reais per month from the state is not enough to pay for the gas, plus the CTA has taken my moto away, "for repairs," they said.

I'm paid for four hours per day, 20 hours per week, but the fact is the work is all day long. You don't have days off or holidays. When people come to me it's Saturday night, Sunday at dawn, saying that this teacher or that community needs help. And once I'm in the seringais, I work all the time. You can't stop after a few hours. I stay a minimum of three days when I make a trip. I'm going to have to begin going again because of the need. People are coming almost daily asking me to help the teachers. Somehow, I have to get my moto back so I can make my visits. As it is, I supplement my salary by repairing old shotguns, and perhaps I can do more of that.

As you know, we don't just teach reading and writing in our schools; we also teach people how to respect each other. We start with interfamilial and social relationships, the idea that we are all equal and that no one has the right to mistreat another. We still have the rare case in which, if you go to the house, the husband is very brusque and will not allow you to talk to his wife, but where you have a school this no longer exists. Things have changed so much; for example, we have almost an equal number of women and men as teachers, some are husband and wife as well. And there are wives who come to Xapuri to participate in the courses and who stay 15 days or a month, and there is no problem with the husband. When we see problems, we talk with the people involved to see if things can be resolved, but if, for example, the husband absolutely refuses for his wife to be chosen as a teacher, then usually she conforms to his will. It also has happened that the wife receives a contract and earns more than her husband, who then makes her quit working. Those are concrete examples that show we still have a long way to go, but we have also made great progress in moving toward gender equality.

Projeto Seringueiro has helped bring about significant improvements in how seringueiros live, see the world, and treat each other. Chico Mendes was the reason that Projeto Seringueiro existed. He and Mary Allegretti were the sustaining forces. I talked about both Chico and Mary in the study I did on Projeto Seringueiro for my degree. I have just finished my degree, but the most wonderful university for me has been the natural university of life—in particular, my experiences working with students and teachers in the seringais of Xapuri.

Dercy Teles de Carvalho

My participation in the rural movement took place as a result of the liberation theology that inspired me and so many others during the 1970s and 1980s. I started when I was about 20 years old as a monitor of an evangelization group in my community, where I still live today, seringal Boa Vista, colocação Pimenteira. Then I became a union delegate from the same community. This was when the union was founded, so you can see I was there from the beginning of both the base communities and the union. I spent a lot of time receiving training in community work

Dercy Teles de Carvalho

and visiting communities, doing capacity building with them, and visiting the parish priests in all the neighboring communities. Padre Cláudio Deustro, who is now in Rondônia; Otávio Deustro, who later married and now lives in São Paulo; and Dom Moacyr, who was the bishop and overall inspiration for the church in this area, and who provided a great example for all of us. Back then, the padres left the altar in order to participate in the communities. It was a great moment for the poor populations who had been oppressed for so long, and for the creation of popular organizations.

The rural movement in Xapuri owes a tremendous amount to the church, which inspired and motivated us. The sociopolitical formation that the church here in Xapuri promoted through its courses and leadership training seminars was absolutely invaluable to all of us. They were taught by people of renown in the history of the movement, like padres Clodovis and Leonardo Boff, Carlos Mestre, Nilson Mourão, who were all activists in the base communities at that time. These individuals were fundamental to the learning process because they imparted a positive, salutary formation that saw the organization of workers as essential for the common good. The concept of individualism was greatly diminished, and the community was always put foremost by the base communities and the church. This was extremely important for the organization of workers and the creation of the unions, and as a result of these capacity-building and leadership workshops for workers, we were discovering other needs that had to be addressed. One of them was education.

To improve their level of information and preparation, and to enable them to participate meaningfully in society, the seringueiros had to become literate. One source of the idea was Mary Allegretti's research with seringueiros in the Upper Juruá River. That experience demonstrated to her the importance of literacy and of using Freire's methodology because he was already famous for his work. I had seen the need here, but I didn't know where to go with it. Mary knew how to put the idea into practice because of her research. She and a group of Freireian intellectuals from São Paulo, CEDI, were key people in getting Projeto Seringueiro going.

The main purpose of literacy was to facilitate the growth of the organization—that is, the union. Radio was very limited at that time. Not that many people had a radio, and the written word was the only way to disseminate information about meetings. Since people couldn't read, it was difficult to communicate. You had to go door to door, which is virtually impossible in the seringal, and publicize meetings. Reading would enable an easier exchange of information and facilitate strengthening the organization. The second purpose of the school was to further cooperation and the cooperative. We had created the cooperative, but you had to read and write in order to carry out any initiative or transaction.

The beginning was fantastic because we opened the schools with the participation of the entire community. Everyone came with palm, construction materials, and their labor to help build. Afterward they contributed food, because seringais are far from each other and people couldn't have a traditional workday like in the city. Community members took care of all these things, and in spite of many obstacles, we got people reading and writing a balance sheet in six months. Ronaldo and Marlete Lima de Oliveira, Fátima, my former husband Manoel Estébio da Cunha, and Armando Soares Filho, we were the pilot team of Projeto Seringueiro, together with Eloisa Winter and Mary Allegretti, who worked more in the urban area as advisors. Learning to read made a big advance in the quality of life of the workers because seringueiros were able to transform themselves into teachers, many of whom are now studying at the university. What's more, we now have students of these first teachers who are also attending university.

While the schools progressed, the question of the cooperatives and health work both regressed; actually under the dictatorship it was better. You see, even though we had a right-wing military government, we also had talented people like Paulo Klein, who was a seminarian who devoted himself to community health. He became a doctor of nursing; he lives in Rio Branco today. He did capacity-building work that formed dentists who helped relieve health problems of the community where people lose their teeth very young because of poor diet and hygiene. Paulo helped by extracting teeth, because toothache is horrible, and he trained people who could also do extractions. There was never one single problem. No one ever administered medicine badly or performed a bad extraction. Still, all this had to end because the Ministry of Health no longer permits those who have no certificate to practice, and in order to get a certificate you have to take a course at the university level, and no one could, so the program ended. There was no follow-up work to help these people get their certificates like there is for the rural lay teachers who got theirs. The state really derailed the health education that we were providing as part of Projeto Seringueiro.

Nor was the state concerned with education for creating critical citizens. They were just concerned with expediting certificates for lay teachers, many of whom used the inappropriate methodology of the urban zone. These, of course, were not Projeto Seringueiro teachers, but other rural teachers who had not been taught how to take into account the rural setting and that you need a different class attendance schedule and method. Now it is different with Binho because he understands the need for a different education for rural areas. The problem is not Binho Marques, but rather the government as a whole. You know, there are many people who are just taking home a paycheck and who are not even interested in rural education, much less committed to it.

I worked in Projeto Seringueiro for five years. My function was to accompany the schools and hold meetings with teachers, like Manoel Estébio and Armando did. Afterward, we would meet as a team and try to identify and solve problems we had observed. Mostly they were conflicts stemming from the lack of formation of the teacher, or conflicts within the community. Going from individualism, which seringueiros were accustomed to, to thinking of the well-being of the group was very difficult, so I tried to help them solve problems in their day-to-day work.

After 1985 I went to work for the union, in the interior of the state of Amazonas, in the municipality of Carabalí, for three years working with Manoel Estébio in the Base Education Movement (Movimento de Educação de Base, MEB). In Carabalí I did the same work I had done here, except that the population there consisted mostly of riverbank farmers and Indians. There the transformation was a lot slower than here; for example, after 20 years of effort the Base Education Movement was able to convince only two farmers to introduce rice and beans into their cultivation. What's more, those two didn't consume the products themselves but sold them! You continued to have fish and *farinha* [ground manioc flour] if you went to eat at their home! That gives you an idea of the pace at which things change.

After that, I worked in Rio Branco for several years at the Fundação Cultural, then I returned to Xapuri and worked for three years, from 1994 to 1997, in cooperative education, helping keep the cooperative going. Then I returned to my home colocação in the seringal and have been there for 10 years now, 1997 to 2007, with no desire at all to go back to the city, even Xapuri.

For a while I worked as part of Xapuri mayor Júlio Barbosa's team, but I became very disenchanted with his administration. Lately, I have worked only in the rural zone in preventive health, which was, of course, part of the original Projeto Seringueiro's founding purpose. It's hard to see advances because it is difficult to change people's habits. It seems to me that things like diet and hygiene are slow to change because they touch our personal habits. Also, many seringueiros think that since their parents lived this way, why should they change? And though many people are well aware of the importance of environmental considerations, there are still some who, when you talk about how the environment is related to their health, and how the burnings ruin the water and the air, they regard you disdainfully, rejecting what you say. They burn because there is still no other technique for them to use to clean the area for planting.

The government has tried to offer some incentives lately, but we have been needing this for over 20 years. Long ago, they should have had technical agrarian workers showing the people alternatives to burning and how to implement them, how to clean an area that they are going to plant now, and how to save an area for the future. People have land, but they do not have the know-how or the materials they need to be successful. The traditional system is very rudimentary and short-term only; it is only about producing now, not about improving the soil. The government needs to make minimal mechanization available immediately. The program Proambiente would do what I'm talking about, but it's not a government initiative. The government is not yet doing anything to address the relationship between rural health and the environment. Just a few NGOs are working in that area. The popular government of Jorge Viana was good in many ways, but it could've accomplished more in the rural sector.

I have become disillusioned with the local government here in Xapuri in recent years because some people talk in the name of the workers but benefit personally. The finances of the union are a mess, the union has debts, nothing is regularized. That is what I am helping out with now, with difficulty, trying to get the records straight, because I'm the only person who understands how to put things back in order. I'm trying to teach others how to keep the records, but I wish I had someone to provide consulting for me! What happened was that the government in Xapuri was co-opted by a small group who lost their ethical sense, lost sight of the fact that we are here to help the workers.

What had given us the collective experience, the education, training, the conscientization, the critical and ethical sense to think of the common good were the base communities. And the Projeto Seringueiro schools came out of the base community experience. The schools were so good because we were absolutely clear about our purpose, our ethics, our principles, and we educated people to question; that's why many of those who have been involved with Projeto Seringueiro have gone on to become leaders. The base communities created us, but we also created ourselves as we created the Projeto Seringueiro schools. It was extremely positive and purposeful.

The problem is that some people now in the Xapuri government have been co-opted because power is a giant monster. You have to have great clarity and your feet firmly on the ground in order to resist its pull. I began to question things, but the motto was "play the game, defend the wrong as right and the right as wrong." I didn't understand how people

I'd known for 30 years could change so much. I think what happens is that the opposition—which is what the PT was for a long time—once it comes to office, its objective becomes staying in office, continuing in power. Then it ends up being just like all the others.

The only way to change society is to start very early with education, so we can create informed, engaged citizens who can organize and exert pressure to force politicians to respect all segments of society. This is the only way to keep change from being co-opted. But when we say, "We won! The government is ours, but we can't criticize because the government is now ours"—that's the beginning of the end. We have won the battle but lost the war.

Part of the ethical problem today has to do with individualism and consumerism, which go hand in hand. Take individualism, for example. I am currently mediating a dispute in the union, a conflict between two seringueiro families. The other day they were showing me a plan of the land; it is so tiny, I couldn't believe they were fighting over it. How can two families fight over such a minuscule piece of property? It's ridiculous! I told them they should both conserve and not plant pasture, which destroys the forest, but they think I'm nuts, and they each want to prevail over the other.

Another thing that worries me is the issue of the sugar cane plantations for ethanol for biofuel, and the so-called management of forest products. The word "management" is a farce, what it is is the removal of wood, not management. We are in a phase where they are blatantly deforesting more and more in the Amazon. What really upsets me are the people of the region who live with nature and know that this so-called management and the sugar cane plantations are completely unsustainable, but who go along with it anyway. It is a negligence of knowledge, not a lack of knowledge. If we don't contain this destruction of the environment, we are going to do away with Amazônia. The situation is more grave every day. I was recently in a public forum on the environment in Acre, and the forecasts are very grim. We know that icebergs are melting and polar bears are threatened, but we are also losing the Amazon. *Fazer sem Agredir* (Develop without Harming), Acre's motto, was just a motto. The government must take the lead and educate permanently, including sponsoring documentaries like Al Gore's *An Inconvenient Truth*.

Everything we've been talking about has to do with education, from the literacy programs of Projeto Seringueiro to health work, to the relationship between health and environmental sustainability. Education is the most important thing. I was born and raised in the Pimenteira seringal, which I hope never to leave, and I will always be grateful that my father thought it important for us to be educated. My father was a northeasterner who came here from Ceará during World War II. He knew how to read and write some; I wouldn't say that he was really literate, even though he did know somewhat the four math operations and he could sign his name. He taught all four of us children to read and write.

With that background and the formation from the church in the base communities, I broadened my knowledge and completed the equivalent of secondary school. Because of financial considerations, I could not go on to the university, and I confess, I didn't want to live in the city [Xapuri] either. The government program Pro-formação is just for teachers, and since I am a health worker and community organizer, I am not eligible. I would be accepted by the private university, but you have to pay and I can't. The mayor's office of Xapuri pays my salary as a health worker, a very small amount: 380 reais per month, minus the withholdings.

When I learned to read and write, it was something that stayed with me forever, as did the desire always to keep on learning. It opened my eyes to the world. My father read a lot in the seringal; he worked in the headquarters, closer to the city, where there were newspapers that the patrão would bring back to use as wrapping for packages. My father would make his purchases, come home and unwrap them, put together the pieces, and read the newspaper. The rubber estate owner had business in Belém where he would travel often and return with many packages; my father would collect all that wrapping paper and read it. The news was about six months out of date, but that didn't bother him; he would always discuss what he was reading with us. That facilitated opening the world up to us. I was the one with the greatest facility for assimilating social and political issues. My father was a thoughtful person; he was of the Conservative Party, but he had a critical mind. He died when I was 20, and it was a great personal loss.

People always ask me, "How can a woman who grew up in the seringal in a machista society overcome the barrier of sexism?" I always answer that it seems to have come naturally for me. In my own family, after my father's death, I became the thinker, the administrator, the payer of debts, the decision maker. I was different from my brothers and sister from the beginning; I always had independent ideas and was not afraid to express them.

The base communities came before Projeto Seringueiro and helped shape it. For me, the late 1970s were wonderful years to be active in the base communities because of the juncture of faith with the needs and issues of the time. The substitution of cattle raising for the traditional seringais, the expulsions, burnings, violence—this was the situation. The big thing for me was discovering that heaven and hell are right here on this planet, and that religion has to be practiced here and now. I can't just prepare myself spiritually. I'm certain that I have a mission to complete on earth, and I need to use my time here to help my neighbor and improve society. I'm convinced that I have to do my part, it doesn't matter if someone at my side is doing the opposite, I have to keep doing what I think is right. You can believe in God and not necessarily be in church. When I am in the seringal, it is like being in a cathedral.

This is where I belong, doing health and community work and defending the forest. In the seringal, I have the opportunity to reflect upon my life, on how the base communities first inspired me and prepared me for my work with the union and Projeto Seringueiro. As I reflect, I am also well aware that I have my father to thank for whatever I may have accomplished thus far.

Antonia Pereira Vieira

I was one of the first Projeto Seringueiro teachers. There was an initial meeting many years ago that I couldn't attend because I had malaria and had to go to the city for treatment, but at that meeting people from the community nominated me, saying I would be a good first-grade teacher. I accepted happily and started doing mini-courses, holding meetings to talk about education, and that's how I got started in Projeto Seringueiro. I lived in the seringal Cachoeira, colocação São Luis.

In the first meetings, people talked about the difficult situation of the seringueiro, and

Photo by author.

Antonia Pereira Vieira

how we needed to educate ourselves in order to overcome the threats to our existence. We teachers were given the first *Poronga,* which contained Portuguese, math, science, and geography all in the same text. I always worked from that text, relating everything to the seringueiros' life and environment. For example, if we wrote the word *"mata"* [forest], we would talk about vowels and syllables, but we would also talk about our life in the forest and how important it is to preserve our culture and habitat. We had children and adults in the same class because parents brought their children; most students had never picked up a pencil, only a few could sign their name. After they were comfortable with pencil and paper and we had learned a bit more, students began to draw birds and trees, copying some of them from the text. But the book was in black and white, while the colors of nature were brilliant, so at a meeting we suggested adding some color to *Poronga,* which the Projeto Seringueiro team did in later editions.

The work was very difficult physically. The school was a one hour walk from my house, and I was often carrying supplies and food to and from home. When I had to take workshops, I had to leave my husband and family to make the trip to Xapuri. I had to make my family understand that it was for my good, their good, and that of the community as a whole that the seringueiro learn to read and write. When I would come here to Xapuri, there was a wonderful person who would always substitute for me in Cachoeira, Duda Mendes. We worked together for many years. Today, I have students who are now teachers in Cachoeira; there's one girl who had the hardest time learning to make her letters correctly, but we worked and worked together, and she improved so much that she is now a teacher there, too.

I've accompanied the entire process of evolution of the school and the union in Cachoeira and in Xapuri for over 25 years now. Years back when she first was union president, Dercy Teles asked me to be a union delegate. I talked it over with my husband, and the next day I accepted, serving for a period of seven years at that time. I was also a teacher in Projeto Seringueiro and a monitor of the church, all three things simultaneously.

When I began as a church monitor, people here knew very little about religion, almost nothing, they had no awareness. But we went to church, to meetings, we began to learn things and wake up from our slumber. I would bring items that we needed, such as food, which was very important as meetings were long and meals were otherwise unavailable or too expensive, and then I would meet with the children. I always invited parents to attend, too, and most of them did. Whether it was to be with their children, have a good meal, or because they were interested in Bible study themselves, I don't know, but they were there. I have spent many, many years as a church monitor and, until recently, as a union delegate also. But I had to quit my union activities because I now have to take care of my father, who is ill and lives with me.

Projeto Seringueiro was active like the base communities and the union. We did not just sit behind desks and dictate a class. No sir! We raised the level of consciousness of the students and the entire community. My daughter is following in these same footsteps now. My desire to do this kind of teaching comes from within myself, first of all. It's part of who I am. Second, I was definitely conscientized by the union activities in defense of the seringueiros; I participated in numerous empates with Chico Mendes, and they have left an imprint on me. I love the community, and even today, though I am no longer an active union delegate, when there are conflicts I try to mediate them, get people to talk about their problems.

Chico Mendes had great confidence in my work in all three areas: the school, the base community, and the union. He became president of the union after Dercy; the two of them worked very well together, and I worked closely with them also. Chico created many schools. He was convinced of the need for more schools, and was always pushing for them. One time, I remember that he presented a proposal, and those funding it asked him, "Do you want the money or the three schools you requested?" Chico immediately answered, "The money!" With the funds for three schools, he built 20 because he had the knack of working with people. People would say, "I'll contribute gasoline," "I'll contribute wood," "I'll bring food," and volunteers also came from outside the community to help with everything. We brought materials in by oxcart and built the schools. We were studying, building, having meetings, educating. It was a time of great unity and a strong sense of purpose. Everyone loved Chico. He knew how to work with the community, get things done, and how to get people to work together, even those who didn't like each other. Representatives from various communities would come and say, "We need a school," and Chico would have a school built, even if it was only for four or five children at the start, because he was convinced that the schools would guarantee our future. He believed that more schools meant more literacy, and that meant stronger popular consciousness and political participation; meanwhile, the communities kept on improving.

Many of the Projeto Seringueiro teachers participated in the empates. There was a very important and dangerous one at Cachoeira, and people from nearby communities all came to help us. They came from Nova Esperança, São Miguel, and Equador seringais, and the teachers from those areas also came and stood in solidarity with us against the ranchers. The people were very united then. We don't have that kind of unity now, but we need to create it again because the forest is once more endangered.

When I was widowed, I came here to live in the town of Xapuri, and I also helped my daughter out when she was taking her exams. She, too, is inspired by the same influences that have motivated me: religion, the union, but especially environmental work. She's married to Nilson Mendes, who is a second Chico, and is very environmentally oriented. This environmental consciousness is also in our curriculum, the newspaper, the radio—and the oral newspapers read on the radio spread the environmental word, too. Nilson gives numerous talks, and hands people material to take home so they will remember the message and tell others. This community has had its environmental consciousness raised over many years, and the message is sticking. Young people pick up trash after they have a party, for example. They clean up everything because we teach them that they have to respect the environment. They have to protect the threatened forest rivers and tributaries, work against deforestation—and Nilson gives talks on all these things because people come here to Xapuri to work and to learn. We've had severe environmental crises, including fires that you can see from airplanes, dense smoke that blocks the sun. Terrible! Because of our history, people are more careful now; well, most are, some aren't. We have to be vigilant and teach young people how important conservation is, because there are powerful forces threatening to destroy the forest for business interests.

In the beginning of Projeto Seringueiro, we talked about reading, writing, the union, and the cooperative in our classes; it was a time of struggle against evictions and burnings. Chico was the one who defended the environment, but now it is everyone, the whole community. Students from the interior are now studying here in Xapuri because there is nothing for them after the fourth grade. It is good for them to come here, learn more about the environmental message, and then share it when they return to the forest.

Binho Marques has been a great help to our schools and communities. You know, he came here many years ago with Chico to my little school in the heart of seringal Cachoeira, and spent 25 days in my house working and learning about Projeto Seringueiro. Governor Jorge Viana was here, too. Both were always supportive.

When I did my elementary and secondary studies, I would come to the town of Xapuri to study during vacations, usually during the month of July. The Encontros they had for teachers were wonderful! In 2001 I began my university course in pedagogy, and I finished last May 2006, like Ademir Pereira, in the same program in Xapuri. I did my project on the environment. In Cachoeira, I taught mostly fourth to sixth grade, but here in Xapuri I teach preschool, four to six years old. I had completed grades one through four myself when I first started teaching in Projeto Seringueiro.

Everything I have participated in has left its influence—the struggle for the land through the empates, the church, the union, my twenty-five years of teaching, environmentalism—and now I am passing them all on to my daughter and my colleagues. I'm positive, and I try to pass on positive energy to my students and others. They have been receptive, so I am hopeful for the future.

I used to pay for the meal for students and teachers with my own funds, prepare it, and make many trips carrying everything on foot a long way when we were just starting Projeto Seringueiro. It was a sacrifice, but it was for the common good and that was very gratifying. Now we have the meal provided, filtered water, electricity. It is so much easier, we have places for our meetings, we have a road and motos. It is much easier to participate now, and people do; when Nilson speaks on the environment, or when I speak, people attend.

I have learned so much from the workshops that
Seringueiro has given for teachers. They would have p
and talk to us about new ways to teach, dynamic activi
involved in learning. Then I would go back and try
own teaching what they had taught us. The most valuable aspects of ___
encontros (workshops) were friendship, collegiality, the exchange of ideas,
meeting new people, teaching others, and learning from them. We all
copied each other; the exchange of ideas was very exciting! The people
who came to direct the workshops gave us individualized attention and
excellent ideas, very appropriate to our situation.

The state still sponsors workshops. Here in Xapuri people have the
time to attend; in the rural zone it is more difficult, and they hold training sessions only two or three times a year. The school encontros usually
last a week, while the church ones are for three days to prepare the monitors. I'm still a monitor; I don't want to give that up.

Church monitors in those three days learn the songs to pass on to
the community. They read and discuss Bible passages, work in groups,
make posters, send meeting announcements on the radio, and then when
they return to their communities, they hold meetings there to spread
the word of God. It is very educational and spiritually uplifting, and
many people attend. A large number of monitors are former Projeto Seringueiro teachers or students of former Projeto Seringueiro teachers.

Projeto Seringueiro has had a profound influence in the community. It was a big entity here, teaching people who today are doing important things. But then it failed. Well, you could say it failed, or you
could say that the knowledge that came from Projeto Seringueiro has
extended outward. The ideas, ethics, and methodology behind Projeto
Seringueiro are now everywhere, in former students and teachers. Education is still raising consciousness, and Projeto Seringueiro continues in
those individuals who began and supported it. Many people in the secretary of education's office, for example, are from the early years of Projeto Seringueiro, and they continue its main lines. They just do it a little
differently now.

Today the most important thing is to study the environment. Both in
the city and the interior, we all need to realize that nature gives us life. We
have to continue raising public awareness on the issue of deforestation and

the need for sustainable activities; this is crucial for our own future. We need to learn not to destroy, but to live and let live, to live in peace. A commitment to the defense of the forest was fundamental to Projeto Seringueiro; we have renewed that commitment today because of the serious environmental threats we are once again facing. ❧

5

Reformers

Introduction

The following voices belong to two very different individuals who have collaborated as friends and colleagues, who worked at different times for CTA/Projeto Seringueiro, and who offer differing perspectives on the history and contributions of the project. One observes clear areas of disagreement between Binho Marques and Pingo Ferreira, the result of inevitable tensions in Projeto Seringueiro's evolution over time. The first voice is that of Arnóbio "Binho" Marques Júnior, formerly director of CTA/Projeto Seringueiro, later secretary of education for Acre, and, since the interview, governor of Acre. Marques, who received a degree in public administration through a partnership between the Universidade Federal do Acre (UFAC) and the Universidade Federal do Rio de Janeiro (UFRJ), has always been an active proponent of education for all, which was his motto and objective as secretary of education.

Marques's interview reminds us of the centrality of the tense political context in which Projeto Seringueiro unfolded during the 1980s, the important role that Chico Mendes played in charting its peculiar direction, and the serious blow that his assassination dealt the project and the entire social movement. Good-humored and frank, Marques recounts how he presided over the death and rebirth of the project and how Project Rubber Tapper influenced his larger educational vision for Acre. In the process, Marques offers important observations on the changing role of NGOs once a socially responsible government takes office.

Djalcir "Pingo" Ferreira, our second voice, joined CTA/Projeto Seringueiro's educational team a few years before Marques left to become

85

secretary of education, and thus oversaw a different phase, which one could describe either as the demise or the institutionalization of Project Rubber Tapper. Either way, Ferreira is an educator committed to excellence. Having spent his childhood in the seringal and his university years in São Paulo where he studied with Paulo Freire, Ferreira knows intimately both the culture of the forest and that of the city. This knowledge is a major theme of his interview and of his rationale for a forest-based curriculum, special teacher-training courses, and follow-up accompaniment. One can feel Ferreira's energy and passion for teacher education, and his dedication to the seringueiros and their culture throughout his interview. Since the interview, Ferreira has accepted Marques' invitation to join the Secretary of Education's Rural Education section.

Binho Marques's and Pingo Ferreira's accounts provide the continuity we need to fill in previously poorly or undocumented spaces in Projeto Seringueiro's history, to learn more about the influence of Chico Mendes, Freire, and Marx, and to appreciate more fully Projeto Seringueiro's checkered trajectory. Let us now turn to two voices that speak to us from their own experience on the theme of education and empowerment.

Arnóbio "Binho" Marques Júnior

For me, the story of Projeto Seringueiro is closely linked with that of Chico Mendes because he is the one who brought me on board. I first met Chico Mendes in 1982 or 1983. I was studying for my university degree and

Photo by Sérgio Vale.

Arnóbio "Binho" Márques Júnior with Ashaninka Indians, Marechal Thaumaturgo.

conducting research on the history of the settlement of Acre. The research, of course, included the rubber tappers, and that's how I met Chico Mendes. Júlia Feitosa, later president of the CTA, introduced me to him in Xapuri. I had had this idea that Chico Mendes was probably a very reserved, serious person, so I was surprised when I met him because he had this warm, expansive manner; he loved to talk and delighted in telling stories. This was not exactly the profile I had of a leader, who I thought would be formal and serious.

At first the seringueiros were fearful, because I had a camera and they thought I was from the federal police. When they saw that I was not, Chico loosened up and he told me a story. One time, he said, he went hunting and he was waiting in a tree, in a spot where the animals came to eat. Suddenly there appeared a deer, but when he aimed at the deer, it began to grow, and it grew and grew until it was enormous, and Chico became frightened and ran away. He said that's how our fears are, they grow before our eyes and overtake us. I truly didn't have the slightest idea what he was talking about; I thought it absurd that an adult would think in that way and believe such stories. I didn't know if he was joking, playing; I didn't get anything.

A few years later, in 1984, I graduated from the university and began to develop a close personal and political relationship with Chico. He was a member of the Workers Party, and I was a member of a clandestine organization, the PRC, Revolutionary Communist Party. Chico was also a member, he belonged to both. The PRC thought it was going to bring about a big revolution. We were earnest Marxist materialists, and we took ourselves very seriously in the PRC. Since Chico was also of my party, I figured that he thought like I did, and when it was time for a party meeting to begin, I assumed that he would show up on time and stick to the agenda. What a naïve expectation! I can't think back on it now without laughing. He and his friends would arrive one or two hours late. The meeting did not have the slightest bit of discipline or order like you would expect of a party meeting, but rather it followed the rhythm of the seringueiros. The tasks that had been set were not completed; nothing was as it was supposed to be according to the plan. At that point, I began to realize that the problem was not the seringueiros, but the plan—that the party's model was totally unrealistic for our culture.

In 1986 Projeto Seringueiro was in a time of great crisis. Ronaldo and Marlete Lima de Oliveira had already left. Only Fátima and Armando Soares Filho remained, and Chico was upset with them because he thought they were moving too slowly, that they were not giving sufficient attention to Projeto Seringueiro. The fact is that Projeto Seringueiro was born as a very small experiment and for a limited purpose. It was born with the cooperative because education was a necessity of the cooperative. There was the school, and the members of Projeto Seringueiro were the teachers. Projeto Seringueiro was not born with a broad-reaching educational purpose, but rather for a locale in seringal Nazaré. Later, seringueiros requested more schools in other places, and that's when we began to train teachers.

There was one school in 1981, three around 1983 or 1984, and eight when I arrived in 1986. During the early years, Projeto Seringueiro was supported by NGOs, mainly Oxfam, then CESE (Coordinadora Ecuménica de Serviços), an ecumenical NGO, which consisted of the Catholic Church and six mainline Protestant churches. When I entered in 1986, Oxfam was no longer providing financing, just CESE. The financial participation of the Catholic Church, through the National Bishops' Council (CNBB), was practically nil, but their presence helped attract other churches—Methodist, Presbyterian, and Lutheran, for example—through the World Council of Churches. Chico did not have much of a relationship with Dom Moacyr because Chico was not a fan of the Catholic Church. He admired Dom Moacyr and supported the base communities and the church's lay leadership courses, but he didn't like the official church itself. If it had been possible, he would have preferred not to have anything to do with the church as an institution. Dom Moacyr, however, was an extremely influential figure who supported and defended the seringueiros every step of their journey.

Through 1982 CPI, the Comissão Pro Indio [Pro-Indian Commission] also helped a bit. Beginning in 1982 FUNARTE, which was part of the Ministry of Culture of Brazil, began minimal financing; this was during the last years of the military government, and the Ministério da Cultura helped up until 1985, after which they said that the experience should be borne by the state secretary of education. About that time Mary Allegretti was saying that our role was to show that forest schools are viable and should become public policy. But Chico Mendes didn't believe that would happen. Instead, he pressed to increase the number of schools; he did not trust the government because of his own personal experience. But the Brazilian Ministry of Culture pressured the state to act, and in 1985 the state of Acre agreed to begin paying the teachers. Projeto Seringueiro trained the teachers, *acompanhava* (accompanied them), carried out field visits and ongoing support of teachers, and the government paid the teachers' salary.

In 1985 Projeto Seringueiro invited me to give a course to the teachers. I remember during the workshop the coordinating team talked to the teachers of the eight schools—that's about 16 teachers, two per school—explaining to them that their schools would soon become part of the public network, and preparing them for that transition. Only what happened was that the schools fell between the cracks. The government did not take charge and neither did Projeto Seringueiro, which had no funds and virtually no staff. This period was marked by the abandonment of the schools. No one was in charge. The teachers used unfamiliar teaching materials made available by the government, with no preparation, and they began to teach their own way, any way they could. And Projeto Seringueiro practically did not exist anymore.

Funding had always been precarious, just bits and pieces from NGOs at the beginning; then from the national Ministries of Culture and Education, not enough to guarantee stability, much less growth. Projeto Seringueiro had no funding when it was turned over to the state, and then, just as Chico had expected, the state government failed to carry out its responsibilities. Chico Mendes became angry, and in an attempt to avoid losing education altogether for the seringueiros, he threw out what was left of the old Projeto Seringueiro team and called me to come in. I called Fábio Vaz, who was Marina Silva's husband, to help me, and the two of us in 1986 basically started Projeto Seringueiro up all over again. Fátima and Armando had gone, and Projeto Seringueiro had only existed because of them. I immediately started reading reports to learn the history of the project, what it used to be like, I listened to tapes, conversed with people trying to piece together the whole story. This was at the very end of 1986.

The first year I was in charge, 1987–1988, Projeto Seringueiro grew from eight to 40 schools! You may wonder how a moribund Projeto Seringueiro could be resuscitated like that. It's simple. The numbers exploded because that's what Chico wanted. In fact, that is what he had always wanted—more schools—and he had not been able to get this growth with previous teams, not did he trust the government, so that's why he brought me on board. Of course, it was impossible to maintain and train teachers, but we forged ahead anyway. I think he figured it was either expand or risk losing everything the seringueiros had gained in education. At any rate, that's what Chico wanted.

We would go to a community to hold a meeting, and I would carefully prepare a number of agenda items to discuss. We would arrive, and Chico would say, "Let's talk about building a school here." He would communicate this to the group in his engaging manner. People were always very enthusiastic, and I would tag along behind with my useless agenda. He wouldn't just promise things, however; no, Chico would follow through, and see to it that the schools were built. Meanwhile, I would still be bringing up the rear. I have to laugh at how little I knew then; now, of course, I understand why Chico wanted so many schools despite the problems such growth would cause.

I had been a teacher in the public system, and I knew very well what worked and what didn't in that network. I knew that the Secretariat of Education at that time absolutely did not function, and that the only way to get anything done was through intermediaries, personal contacts. Everything was completely informal, and I had learned whom to talk to in order to get anything accomplished in the state system. Chico wanted me to use my knowledge of the system to resurrect Projeto Seringueiro and help him build more schools.

In 1987 we did a project with the Ministry of Education and Culture (MEC) in which we built 12 schools; the little school in Cachoeira is one of them. It has two rooms, a walkway, a refectory. It is made from sawn lumber and is very nice. This marks another moment because this is a real seringueiro school. You see, the seringueiros' project was not the project of Projeto Seringueiro.

Allow me to explain. The project of Projeto Seringueiro was to form personnel to direct the cooperative, to strengthen a political consciousness for confronting the ranchers, the dictatorship, the development of Amazônia; this was the project of Projeto Seringueiro, the ideological project. What was the project of the seringueiros? Their project was a formal school, which they did not have. They wanted a true school, just like everyone else had, with first, second grade. They wanted a school for their children, and Projeto Seringueiro's schools were initially for adults. The school in Cachoeira that I mentioned, beginning from the time I entered, began to bring closer together Projeto Seringueiro and the project of the seringueiros themselves. That was the project of Chico Mendes.

Chico wanted real—that is, formal—schools. He pushed the initial ideological phase, but he knew when the first phase was over, when the original Projeto Seringueiro was no more. He could see that there was no longer education for anyone; it was dead. The expansion from eight to 40 schools was what he and all the seringueiros wanted, too, hoping that with the schools would come a true system of education in the forest. That is, in fact, what we did with that expansion: create a system. We gave students the equivalent of the first four years divided into two parts: literacy and postliteracy. It was impossible to control, but Chico felt there was no alternative.

At any rate, I worked very hard to develop a relationship with the Secretariat of Education and explain to them the value of Projeto Seringueiro schools. I understood that it was the obligation of the government to assume the schools, and I committed myself to meeting more and more with the secretary about these responsibilities and how to carry them out: the hiring of teachers, the school lunch, the didactic materials. By working very closely with the secretary of education of Acre, I was able to get them to commit resources for the schools and help them do it.

In 1991 I left to work in CEDE for a year. In 1993 I worked in the mayor's office, with the secretary of education until 1994. In 1999, I assumed the position of secretary of education (1999–2007) of Acre. [Marques became governor of Acre in 2008.] I left CTA/Projeto Seringueiro in 1991—first, because Chico's death in 1988 affected me deeply, and, second, because I disagreed sharply with some members of the leadership of the seringueiros' movement over the direction they were taking. After Chico's death, as you know, many sources of financing appeared from all over to support projects in the rainforest, but the movement itself did not have its own project; rather, the leaders made their project according to the resources that came in. For example, there was a big conflict over a project with Canada, with Canadian cooperation agencies; they had a crazy project they wanted to do, and I disagreed with the coordinators of the National Rubber Tappers Council (CNS) at that time. Things were not going well at all; I was miserable, and we suffered terribly without Chico's leadership.

In 1990 Jorge Viana was candidate for governor and was almost elected; he tried again the next term, but again he was defeated, and after that loss everything seemed hopeless to me. I didn't have any support from the National Rubber Tapper Council leadership; actually I didn't have the support of anyone. I was invited to work for CESE, so I accepted and spent two years there, which I enjoyed very much. Finally, Jorge Viana was elected mayor of Rio Branco. Then things began to change for the better, and I became part of that change. You can see how individuals affect events tremendously; Chico Mendes is the most obvious example, but Jorge Viana is one also. He has been a strong leader for Acre.

When I started at CTA/Projeto Seringueiro, as I said, Projeto Seringueiro was virtually dead, and the CTA existed only on paper; it was just a small room in a space donated by the state government. The CTA had been created in 1983 by Mary Allegretti, but, except for administering Projeto Seringueiro, it had been dormant. I requested a larger room, and in 1987 the CTA began to exist again, with only two people, myself and Fábio; soon Júlia Feitosa came on board, but she was not involved in education. In 1987 or 1988 Júlia invited a friend of hers who had done a master's degree in the Northeast, Reginaldo de Castelo, to join us. This Reginaldo, his doctrinaire Marxist ideas had long ago been left behind by the seringueiros, but he came in here and started having meetings and trying to convince Chico Mendes to arm the seringueiros! This is hard to imagine now, but it's true. Reginaldo came in with a lot of theory, and he began to find my way of doing things too slow, so he said that we had to arm the seringueiros. He actually wanted to start a war! I thought he was crazy, and I was afraid that some of the seringueiros were starting to take him seriously, especially since this was the height of the tension over the land question and the ranchers were using violence against us, and even Chico halfway listened to this guy, so I left Projeto Seringueiro.

In just a few months, Reginaldo was in charge of Projeto Seringueiro. Chico saw that he was a disaster, fired him, and asked me to return. I did, but for a brief, intense time of great crisis because it was 1988, and Chico was murdered that same year. I was very confused and extremely discouraged after that. It was very difficult because Chico Mendes had a great capacity to unify people, while the other leaders in the group lacked that ability altogether. And Chico died poor; he was a person who gave himself completely for a cause; other leaders were more proud, egotistical, our personal relationships were terrible, and I left again.

In 1999 when I became secretary of education, I called the CTA, asking them to help me extend the positive accomplishments of the Projeto Seringueiro experience to the state level, but they decided not to work with the state at that time. Projeto Seringueiro had many failures, but they also had many successes. The one who has been excellent in Projeto Seringueiro is Pingo Ferreira; whatever he does is outstanding, and I very much needed his expertise on my team. But where I was concerned with making education accessible to everyone, Pingo was afraid that the high quality of teacher preparation that he had painstakingly achieved would be sacrificed.

Well, you can imagine what happened. Pingo is a marvelous teacher trainer and an excellent creator of curricula. He absolutely loves staying out there in the forest, he is extremely dedicated, he stays in the school when he gives seminars, he knows all the community members and their children, and they all love him. As a result, the seringueiros would much rather see him coming than the bureaucrat that the state sends out, who stays only briefly and then returns to the city. Of course, Pingo's way is far superior, but I have to provide something for all the schools. Then I visited Colombia and learned of their model, which I am adapting here in Acre to help provide education for all. However, I'm not giving up on Pingo. I want him to come and teach us how to take his experience with excellence and make it public policy.

What was my dream? My dream was to take Projeto Seringueiro's successes statewide, produce a kit, a packaged curriculum, for all the mayors in Acre to see. "Look," I wanted to say to them, "it is possible to train teachers for schools in the seringais." A kit would contain books and other materials. It would help them with guidelines saying, for example, in order to carry out the first through fourth grade successfully, we need this many books, that many teachers trained in this or that way. But the Projeto Seringueiro team didn't want to do this because they thought it would compromise quality.

Pingo works with eight schools now; he chose the best of the 40 and turned the others over to us. He works with the best teachers in the best schools. However, when Projeto Seringueiro began, remember, it began with teachers who were illiterate. They made posters, very elementary materials, these were the real teachers, and all the Projeto Seringueiro teachers were like that. Then they achieved this amazing transformation from illiterate seringueiros to teachers. It was fantastic! Now it is time to do the same thing on a larger scale. The teachers in the other schools are not exceptional; they are average, but they're what we have, and we have to work with what we have.

It is difficult to evaluate the influence of Projeto Seringueiro because it has had such ups and downs. When no government existed, the only schools in Xapuri were those of Projeto Seringueiro, and they fulfilled the basic role amazingly well. Today the government is administering these schools. What should be the role of Projeto Seringueiro today? Indeed, what is the role of any NGO today?

NGOs today have to be very good, or they will not make it. They have an identity crisis now. Before, there was nothing for the people except NGOs, but this government is for the poor. Unfortunately, some NGOs continue working as if the government doesn't exist.

I know from experience how difficult it is being in an NGO. A large part of the problem is funding, not just obtaining funds, but writing the reports to the funding agencies, and different reports stress different things. For example, if you make a report for a European agency, you have to respond to contributors who have a fantastic idea about the third world, and you have to write to please their fantasies, even though they have totally unrealistic ideas about the Amazon. The report may not actually tell you what is really happening, or what is really needed, or important, or wrong with the project.

When I worked at CESE, I saw what a complicated effort it is to get funds to help a poor community. The donor really doesn't want to know too much about that reality; he is moved by the sentiment of wanting to do something to help out. All projects have problems, but the donor doesn't want to hear about problems; he just wants to invest in something halfway exotic, a kind of magical cause. Soon, you have a whole chain of fictions that are built up, and the report gets further and further away from reality, but the report has to please the funders, so it feeds their fantasies. The fictions in the reports are sometimes so well done that the people working on the project receive a prize or a medal on their chest. When that happens, then there's absolutely no way they can admit that their project has any flaws! Chico Mendes never, ever played that game. He always knew how to be himself and how to remain himself, even with medals and awards. Anyone who knew Chico knows this truth. Projeto Seringueiro fell victim a bit to fame when it came, but their main shortcoming was that they didn't know how to deal with their problems and solve them calmly.

With regard to writing funding reports, well, people have to pay the bills at the end of the month, so it is better to tell a pretty story in order to continue surviving and be able at least to help some people in an imperfect program. The relationship between funding agencies and the people on the ground who are carrying out the project is very complicated. When I went to work for CESE, I lived with this conflict because the project was good, but it had problems. If I did a full report detailing everything, it would lose financing, and it was a project of considerable value. In the end, this conflict doesn't help anyone. When NGOs embroider too much, and the visitors come to see for themselves, they are often disappointed. They arrive with such high expectations, but what they see are very poor people who are still poor, and maybe they will decide to stop donating. It is difficult, but you have to do things correctly from the start, or it doesn't do anyone any good.

Doing things correctly also means remembering always that we would have never made it to this office without the seringueiros behind us. We are in the government today thanks to the hard work and sacrifice of those who came before us. That effort is filled with problems and failures, of course, but it got us here. The cooperative has succeeded; yes, there are many problems with it, including people who are corrupt or problematic, but it is also marvelous. The schools of Projeto Seringueiro have succeeded as well; despite the many errors, crises, and times of virtual standstill, they have given the state a model for excellence in rural education.

Djalcir "Pingo" Ferreira

People sometimes ask me what effect Projeto Seringueiro has had on rural education in Acre. That's not an easy question to answer because it has had direct and indirect effects, and it has had an influence outside the classroom, in the family and the community. One example of a direct influence is the partial adoption by the state of our practice of accompaniment. This is something that we have provided to all Projeto Seringueiro teachers because they began as lay, uncertified teachers without schooling, that is, practically illiterate. That's different from the lay

Djalcir "Pingo" Ferreira

teachers whom you have in the city, who have some schooling but no certification. The unschooled lay teachers of Projeto Seringueiro, slowly, with lots and lots of time and commitment on their part and ours, have become very fine teachers. In order to accomplish this objective, we carried out monthlong training courses at different points in the year, which I will discuss later, and then followed them up with systematic accompaniment. The idea is that the school would have a visitor one week per month to work on site with the teachers, but we don't have the staff to do that anymore, so we reduced it to one week every two months, and that has been enough to help teachers gain confidence and skills. The state is now using our accompaniment model, although the observer usually just visits for a few days and then leaves. But at least the state recognizes the importance of the concept. This is because personnel formerly with Projeto Seringueiro like Binho Marques, the secretary of education, and Manoel Estébio da Cunha, and Chiquinha da Silva, who now work for the secretary of education, realize the effectiveness of our model and are adapting it as much as possible to improve supervision of rural teachers.

Despite the difficulties of life in the forest, the exodus to the city is diminishing, people are staying put, and rural education is becoming more and more important. Migration has slowed for many reasons, but at least in some measure because CTA/Projeto Seringueiro has had many conversations with teachers, students, and their communities about the relationship between the city and the forest. The seringueiros understand that the city presents not only many attractions, but also many problems, cultural and economic. The seringueiros' culture is denigrated on a daily basis in the city, their knowledge is not marketable, and unemployment levels are very high. The lure of the city is still strong for the young who think that it represents everything marvelous. In some places with electric power, television has entered the forest, and with it, an aggressive consumerism that targets youth. The seductive urban propaganda put out by the TV is hard to counter, but I think we have raised people's awareness about the pros and cons of the city; this is an indirect influence of Projeto Seringueiro.

Another area where Projeto Seringueiro has been very active in educating, especially by example, is in gender equality. It continues to be a long road because seringueiro culture is very conservative and machista, and though there is an equilibrium between women's and men's social functions, they are mostly determined by gender. In Projeto Seringueiro, we have always treated each other as equals. We divide the tasks, and we don't have this business about this is the woman's job and this is the man's.

This example has been internalized by our teachers, and in the schools where the teachers have discussed this topic well and with tact, there is a notable difference, and the students divide jobs equally. Of course, it all depends on the quality and example of the teacher. Occasionally, there is still some resistance, some parents who don't want their son to do certain tasks at school. For example, over there in Nova Esperança there are parents who don't want their boy to participate in clean-up activities with the others. There are still a few like that, but generally speaking, everyone—teachers and students—does everything in the schools and they divide all the work. We treat the topic of gender and equality with great tact and sensitivity, for although things are changing, change is gradual.

When Binho Marques became secretary of education and Manoel Estébio da Cunha went to work for him, they made a concerted effort to equip Projeto Seringueiro schools with materials, dictionaries, and maps, and with funds provided by international cooperation. They purchased materials appropriate to our students, something MEC, the Ministry of Education of the federal government, has never done. They bought items that we had suggested to assist us in teacher formation, materials that talk about how to study, and how learning takes place, for example. We work with these concepts in our teacher training courses and needed this type of support material. They also purchased grammar texts, maps, dictionaries, and other reference materials, because we have numerous group projects and we use these resources constantly. Many rural schools, unfortunately, lack these materials, but the secretary of education of Acre is trying to supply them to all rural schools; this is another example of the influence of Projeto Seringueiro.

I keep criticizing MEC because they have a one-size-fits-all mentality. The big thing they are pushing now is the *livro pronto,* you know, the prepackaged text kit with accompanying workbooks. It is pretty, colorful, and it is like a fetish among certain groups. Everyone wants a new book each year, so they put out a new edition, but it's the same thing masquerading as something new. We don't need this; we need for teachers to learn how to study and teach.

For example, we always use the *Almanaque Abril,* which is an excellent encyclopedia and is regularly updated with useful entries; this helps teachers learn how to locate information. We also have something similar to the *Mala de Livros,* Projeto Seringueiro's earlier children's literature program that was so successful, that MEC has begun sending us. But MEC's children's literature, like all their materials, is simply delivered to the state secretary of education's office without any funds budgeted for teacher training or any explanation of how to use the texts. That's MEC for you. Good intentions, but very bureaucratic and out of touch with local realities.

Perhaps a good way to judge the contributions of Projeto Seringueiro is to contrast our way of operating with that of MEC. Take, for example, what we did in our teacher training in Xapuri on how to use children's literature. We took lots of time to familiarize teachers with the texts, to make them comfortable with the material. Remember, these are people for whom reading a simple story still presents a challenge. Socorro D'Avila de Oliveira, who worked with us on this, spent 30 days conducting activities on how to comprehend and present the literature. The point is that we had to adjust our time and activities to the "clock" and skill level of the forest people. With Socorro we developed interdisciplinary activities based on the literature that incorporated reading, writing, math, geography, history, and Portuguese. All the while we are teaching skills, but we are also helping teachers establish connections between disciplines, as well as between what they are reading and their students' lives. The teachers have a great need for this kind of preparation, which has been the hallmark of Projeto Seringueiro and the aspect that the state finds most difficult to replicate.

I can't overemphasize the importance of the workshops. The teachers absolutely love them and look forward to them with eager anticipation because it is a time of learning, sharing, and socializing. They go to great lengths to attend. To give you an idea of their dedication, we have one teacher who traveled seven hours on foot just to arrive at the road in Xapuri where she could get a ride to the workshop. With her first paycheck she purchased a pressure cooker to make cooking easier for her family while she was away. With her second one, she bought a horse to facilitate travel from the forest to Xapuri. It's hard for people in the city to realize how different everything is in the forest, the vast distances between communities and the difficulty of travel. This makes for a very different culture from that of the city, and one in which extended workshops are a necessity.

Teachers' Workshop. Xapuri.

It is also helpful to keep in mind that our teachers are all barely literate at the beginning. Everything is new to them, and they have to build skills and self-confidence at the same time. The teacher trainers, the team, have to be very sensitive to that fact. For example, Socorro was working on the production of a booklet of stories that the teachers were writing in their own everyday language. She thought things were coming along nicely until one teacher approached her and confessed, "I'm not going to try this with my students because I'm not confident that I can do it." If you insist, then you damage the teacher's self-confidence, which is fragile to begin with. If he is uncertain of his ability to do something, then he just won't do it; that's why we have to have training and have it according to their time frame. But what MEC does is leave the book with the teacher, provide no training, and say "Here, use this."

Things are made more difficult for our teachers because all reference points are to the city. The forest is another world, and MEC doesn't take this into account. I'll give you an example. One day I was in São Luis do Remanso, and the teacher there was discussing a section on litter from an MEC text, and that you should place litter in wastebaskets. This is totally inappropriate, because in the forest we don't have wastebaskets. That's why I say they don't adjust things to the forest. Another example: I was working over on the riverbank in Xapuri, talking with teachers about an MEC book that has a unit on aquariums and fish. I said to one of the teachers, "Maria, the students don't know what an aquarium is, but you live right here on the riverbank. Why don't you teach them about the fish we have here, in the rivers and streams and ponds." She was very excited about that approach, and her students made a wonderful little booklet that is just about fish. The MEC text was completely designed for the urban student; so, first, you have to contextualize, then you can talk about aquariums. We are working with the teachers to help them make the articulations between the local and the universal, and it is going very well.

On the topic of adapting and valuing the local culture, our own Projeto Seringueiro text, *Educação Matemática na Floresta* [*Math Education in the Forest*], is a good example. I listened for a long time to many forms of local speech, and, with the assistance of the team, created a text based on what I had heard. Though the main focus is math, the text contains sequences that work with science, Portuguese, and geography as well, because the conceptual fields are very broad. The text presents the situation of a person who is walking through the forest observing his surroundings. He knows the name of the trees, the flora and fauna, and the type of animals that live in the ravines, the rivers, the shallows. The students discuss all this, and then the teacher uses the story to help students classify the types of soil, water, trees, and forest animals. Only after he has done that does he present the polar bear from the MEC book. By then, the students are able to go to the map and find the polar bear's habitat, classify it like they did with the local animals, and use its scientific name. This is linking the particular to the universal.

In the process, they locate rivers where these animals live, the Madeira, the Purús, and they discover that Amazônia is not just Brazil. When the teacher does his work well, he does not limit himself to the local, but he begins with the local and places it in the larger world. If the teacher just sticks to the polar bear, the giraffe, which they have on TV and in the circus, the students talk only about the animals that we do not have in Brazil. That type of approach makes the student feel that his surroundings are somehow inferior, so our approach is to say, "Look, here in the forest science exists." Culturally, it is a necessity to link the individual to the place where he lives. If he becomes dislocated, he doesn't understand or appreciate his locale. The problem is that virtually all MEC's materials come from cities like São Paulo and Brasília; there is very little local production of texts. We have been forgotten for over 100 years here in the forest, and it's going to take a long time to overcome that history.

The ministry of education was created by the federal government in 1930; since that time they have never opened their doors to listen to the social movements. They just work with content, that's it: the student takes notes, he doesn't process anything, it's very inflexible and urban. In the forest, people know a great deal, but what they know is not valued by the outside world, including the producers of educational materials, and the seringueiros, in turn, devalue their own culture. It is basic Freireian philosophy to value and build upon what the learner already knows, his local culture and experiences. That's why the little booklets the teachers produced on forest animals and fish are so important. When they see their own stories in their own language, they feel highly valued; they have made a book, which is amazing to them. Then they see that their book is just as good as the material that they get from the city, and it is in their own words. When I took them to see the fish there in the Parque Nacional de Jaú, they were enchanted, because they saw their own text come alive before their very eyes. The booklet is very pretty, the design and descriptions are theirs, and in the park they felt important.

Another example is the booklet *Animals* (*Bichos*), which teaches classification of animals, vertebrates, invertebrates, mammals. It also talks about onomatopoeia—for example, the sound of the *cancão* bird. This is a carnivorous bird; it goes "cancancancão," it is very strident. The *cancão* you will find only in the *mata bruta,* deep in the virgin forest. There are many animals in this booklet that here in the city no one knows what they are. This could provide a wonderful exchange of materials with the city. Teachers learn through this activity that the rivers leave the forest, join up with the Amazon, that the Amazon region includes other countries, and they follow the river's journey until it empties into the ocean. Perhaps they would use these materials more in the city if it weren't for the strict schedule which messes everything up, because this project I'm talking about lasted 30 hours. It consisted of reading, writing, producing the text, and classifying the animals. It was a beautiful project!

The animal stories are the work of the teachers in the training workshop; they then passed the stories on to their students. Everything the Projeto Seringueiro team does is for teachers to communicate to their own classes depending on the degree of confidence they have in their mastery of the material. We have enough Portuguese, math, geography, and science in one small text to last a whole year. That's important because some teachers have both adults and children in the same class, so the idea is to have them all work on the same text. This began to be less of an issue about 1989 or 1990 when the number of students under 15 years of age rose to 60%. By 2005, it was up to 77%.

The schools and the teachers have improved significantly over time; there has been a very positive evolution. Many teachers see growth in the way the seringueiros regard themselves and the world, and I see a growing critical awareness in the teachers. They are feeling more and more like their forest world has value, despite the onslaught of propaganda from the city.

In the math workshops, we work on the four operations, classification, inventory, and correspondences. In order to establish distances and permit reflection on that topic, to train the eye and the ear to observe what is sensory, we do comparison and generalization, it's all Western rationality. When you talk about comparison and generalization, you can open up a dialog between traditional and empirical forms of knowledge because these are two categories that they have in common. In this way, teachers and their students learn about the world that surrounds them, the particular, and they establish a connection with the universal. Here you have inclusion of both the lettered and the oral world.

Our basic ethical philosophy in Projeto Seringueiro is always to ask open questions because they give birth to other questions and to critical reflection. This, too, is very Freireian. This process should not be subordinated to the arbitrary time of the clock.

At one workshop, we did a very interesting exercise involving developed and underdeveloped countries. Teachers consulted the *Almanaque Abril,* which is in all the schools now, to find information on three developed and three underdeveloped countries in order to compare them. They made tables, charts of population, area, GNP, per capita income, literacy index, and human development index. The teachers chose the United States, Japan, Senegal, Angola, Sweden, and Brazil. The relationship between literacy and household income provided an eye-opening comparison for everyone. Further, when teachers saw that the literacy rate for Sweden was practically 100%, they were amazed! The country comparison game is an example of a thought-provoking exercise that was inspired by a game. Ademir Pereira, Socorro D'Avila de Oliveira, and I gave the monthlong course, but now we have neither the money nor the staff for similar workshops.

How we define "literate" and "illiterate" is an ongoing discussion; we have found no complete agreement in the literature, so we created our own standard. If a person can read and write—that is, read a very brief text and describe its contents, write a very brief message, read a letter, and perform the four basic math operations—then that person has demonstrated competency at the first level of literacy. The second phase specifies more detailed competencies, which we have outlined in separate documents.

We use evaluation cards to assess the teachers' performance in the workshops. An interesting category on the evaluation card is "separates what is his from what is not his." This may seem an unusual category, but it is very useful. At first, teachers rated pretty low in that area because they mixed party politics and the school. Xapuri is very, very PT, very, very church. I never have been a member of any political party, I just don't like party politics. What we talk about in school is citizenship, collective rights of ourselves as subjects, not party politics. When I entered the CTA in 1988–89, I couldn't separate what was the church's from what was the PT's from what was the union's. It was so difficult because they were all the same people, and so, naturally, everyone thought that they were all the same thing. Some even thought that the CTA and the government were the same thing. For that reason, it is important in the evaluation card to have this category so that teachers will understand that the public must be separate from the private.

Another category we work on is spelling, but here we have to be very tactful, because the seringueiro spells like he speaks, and correcting his spelling is also correcting his speech. For example, instead of *nós vamos,* the seringueiro says *nós vai;* instead of *nós fomos,* it's *nós fumos;* for *encontro,* he says *encronte;* for *contaminado,* he says *contraminado; caçarola* becomes *caçalora;* and *amarelo* becomes *amalero.* We ask them to pronounce and to read as the word is written. Others in class hear the mistake, and then we ask them to talk about it and then someone goes to look it up. You have to be very careful not to hurt anyone's feeling because once you do that, then it's all over and you lose them, but most of the time, teachers are very eager to write correctly.

Our methodology is Freireian, of course. We use the *A Lição da Samaúma* text, on which I collaborated with the Freireian author Maria Lúcia Martins, as our theoretical base. However, our experience is that there is no completely appropriate theory for the conditions of an overwhelmingly oral culture and for people who have had no history of schooling. Everything is still very incipient. So to Freire, we add some basic Piaget, Vigotsky, Delia Lerner (she works in Argentina and in Venezuela), and each source is a tributary that flows into the broader river. I would say that perhaps 40% of what we do comes from the tributaries; the rest of the "river" are adaptations that we have learned from our own experience with the seringueiros. Thus, what we have done over time is, with the example of our math text, use the seringueiros' culture, including its orality and forest environment, as a basis for learning, and intersperse the practice of numbers, correspondences, and map reading in an effort to create a culture of studying and learning, of reading letters and numbers. We incorporate both systems of representation of reality into our texts and workshops.

In my own education, I have had many powerful influences. I graduated in physics from the Pontifical Catholic University (PUC) in São Paulo. Later, I did a course at the University of São Paulo (USP) in physics and mathematics. I am from Acre, but I went to São Paulo to study because my family knew someone who had gone to São Paulo and who had an inexpensive pension where I could stay. At USP I was overwhelmed by the extent of academic and disciplinary fragmentation; it seemed so unnatural and wrong to me. I wanted to reunite everything, beginning with the sciences—biology, pharmacy, medicine, chemistry, mathematics; they all have so much in common, but specialization fragments everything. In these courses I observed the need to integrate disciplines, and that was one significant influence on me. I began to apply my desire to unify knowledge here in the CTA after I returned to Acre. It was a lot of work because education is very specialized here, too, and people don't want to mix with other areas. This was a struggle, but in our math education, for example, we were able to overcome the usual fragmentation. In addition, I think that we were able in the 1996 version of *Poronga* to express an integrated, interdisciplinary view, and to explain how educational needs in the forest differ from those in the city.

I felt like I had made some small impact regarding specialization when in a 1989 discussion with the teachers and the team, a teacher remarked that they, the teachers, have to work in all areas and be generalists, while the team members, the trainers, all have their specialties. He pointed out the irony that the educated team members can teach only one discipline, while the semiliterate teachers have to work with them all. Everyone had to agree that there was a contradiction there!

I began at CTA at the end of 1988, as I mentioned earlier, and sometimes I laugh and ask myself why, because it has been a struggle, especially these last years. Different friends encouraged me to make the move. You see, when the extractive reserves were decreed, Binho Marques and Jorge Viana, who was working for the semigovernmental organization FUNTAC and now is the governor, invited me to work on an education project for the reserves. At the time I was teaching at the university here (UFAC) and also at the high school. Jorge called me in September 1988 and asked me to leave the high school to assume the new project and also to give a course in December. Graciete Zaire, Andréa Maria Lopes Dantas, Chiquinha da Silva, and I worked on this until April 1989. I had many influences to guide me, in particular my experiences with trying to decompartmentalize areas of knowledge from my university days in São Paulo. So I took the assignment. In the reserves the teachers with whom we have worked in Projeto Seringueiro use our methodology, but those in the state schools in the reserves do not; their model is urban, with exams, schedules.

The law says that all schools have to have a *Projeto Político Pedagógico,* a Political-Pedagogical Project, strategic plan. It is important to have a pedagogical proposal for the forest schools, although most areas didn't take the requirement seriously and the MEC is clueless in the first place, but I worked hard on ours, and there is one for the extractive reserves, too. The State Education Council approved ours, and we hope that it will become a pilot project so that other teachers in the reserves, not just our eight Projeto Seringueiro schools, might adopt this model too. If Projeto Seringueiro held training courses for these teachers, we could teach them in an interdisciplinary way and on "forest time" from the beginning. As it is now, they are schooled in the old way, and if they come to us for a class, we have to try to undo their training. We would like to offer in-service training with pedagogical accompaniment, follow-up on-site. I wrote most of the *Proposta* and the Appendices with the specified competencies at each phase, plus an accompanying handout on the history of Projeto Seringueiro that emphasizes the concrete mode of thought of the seringueiro, his present rather than future orientation, the fundamental environmental basis of forest education, and the long-term effects of isolation and discrimination on the seringueiros' psychology and worldview.

Of course, what MEC wants to give are distance courses with a kit for each module, two hours for this, one hour for that, plus something to do at home. That is too rigid. They think humans are like a computer, but the time of the learner is different from the time of those who make the modular units.

Though I have studied in São Paulo, I know the life of the seringueiro from personal experience because I was born in the seringal Bom Destino in Porto Acre. My father was the bookkeeper in the seringal. He had learned accounting from a Portuguese, *o seu* Lopes, and kept all the books for the seringal. I still have vivid images of the large riverboats that would arrive with goods and supplies, and I remember how eagerly we anticipated their coming. The cargo would be unloaded, and then the boats would depart laden with rubber and Brazil nuts from the seringal. Everything arrived at the headquarters where my father worked registering supplies. It was also very exciting to me to accompany my father when he would travel into the forest with a convoy of burros. It was a delight to be a child in the seringal. We were eight children, and we enjoyed great freedom playing in the trees and the river. Perhaps that is why I love being in the forest so much today. I was sad when my family moved from the seringal to Manaus, where we spent eight years, while my father stayed back in the seringal working. It was in Manaus that I learned how to read and write. Later, we moved to Rio Branco where I spent two years before going to São Paulo to become a pilot. Imagine that! Really what I wanted to do was just explore the world.

In São Paulo, I worked for four years at the *Folha de São Paulo* newspaper at night doing formatting; that job doesn't exist anymore. I soon gave up the idea of aeronautics and studied education while living with a family in their modest pension. Then I thought I would study architecture because I liked design. Finally I tried physics and loved it. Physics helped me get my feet on the ground; it taught me discipline, which was essential because I was all over the place. I developed the practice of studying about 10 hours per day, and I thrived on it.

During my seven years in São Paulo, I had some outstanding professors who influenced me greatly. Luiz Carlos de Menezes, for example, was a physicist who gave very stimulating classes; he was completely Freireian in his methodology. This was during the dictatorship, more or less 1977–83, and he said something to me that determined my direction in life. He told me, "You're doing physics thinking you're going to bring about a revolution, but that won't happen, because all your research will only go to strengthen capital interests. If you really want to bring about a revolution, go into education, into the public schools. Look at our teachers, and you will see the paradigm of precisely what should not be done. This is where change should begin." We students were all against the dictatorship and we wanted to do whatever we could to restore democracy, and Menezes was telling me that chalk was my weapon, to use my head and make a revolution with chalk.

Che Guevara was a big influence on university students during the dictatorship; there was much talk of joining guerrilla groups. In a crackdown by the military, the secretary of security ordered troops to invade PUC's campus; they threw a bomb that started a fire, they destroyed offices and files, and beat and arrested scores of students and faculty indiscriminately. The invasion had a chilling effect in that everyone was shocked, but it did not silence opposition. It seemed that even more exhilarating speakers came from all over Brazil and from other countries to talk at PUC and USP. It was a time of great political effervescence and exciting intellectual exchange. It was a dangerous but stimulating period, because in São Paulo, through lectures, theater, art, and music, democratic ideas were being expressed openly, and everyone was, in their own way, combating the dictatorship.

There were still others in São Paulo who influenced me greatly. Jair Militão at PUC in education gave very inspiring lectures. Paulo Freire was, of course, amazing, and I was very fortunate to be able to study his work with him at PUC after he returned from exile. This was between 1980 and 1982, *a gente fêz um trabalho com êle de analisar a obra dêle* (we

ct with him to analyze his work). I remember many
d to go work in Mozambique, to help out there, but
k in our own country, there is so much to be done. He
ck to Acre and improve things there. He said if I must,
que and see how difficult it is to *fazer revolução* (make a
revo͟l͟u͟t͟i͟o͟n͟) t then come back and work at home. Militão told us the
same thing. In the end, I didn't go to Mozambique.

Menezes is a very impressive person. He's a physicist but he's active
in many other areas as well; he is a founder of the PT. Mário Schemberg
at PUC is the same way, he's a physicist and art critic. Paul Virillo and
Edgar Mohan were other influential intellectuals and militants. Maria
Lúcia Martins, formerly our CTA/Projeto Seringueiro advisor with whom
I did the mathematics training course and whom I assisted in writing
her text, she, too, is very Freireian and she, too, was a militant at that
time who, like the others, had "problems" with Brasília.

All my militant friends deeply desired to improve the whole country. I remember another student, Beatriz Maria, spoke of good citizenship as consisting of three things: (1) exercising a critical sense, (2) taking
a position, (3) being responsible. This is what my friends and the intellectuals who influenced me so much had in common: their seriousness,
dedication, discipline, and desire to change the country. Throughout,
Freire's influence was everywhere.

Everyone in Projeto Seringueiro was deeply influenced by Freire. I
brought all my influences from São Paulo back with me. Projeto Seringueiro had been founded on Freireian principles, but they were reinforced when I came on board. Above all, however, Projeto Seringueiro
has been flexible, always adapting to the realities and culture of the seringueiro. Though we now have virtually no funds and no staff and are at
a crossroads, and though we have had numerous failures and disagreements along the way, we have created a holistic, environmentally based,
consciousness-raising educational program that respects the seringueiro's
universe while bringing him into the broader world. ༫

6

From Projeto Seringueiro to Rural and Indigenous Education

Introduction

The voices in this chapter speak of the importance of political activism, consciousness-raising education, respect for the forest, faith in action, and the values of perseverance, creativity, and a strong personal ethical code to carry one through challenging situations.

Ivanilde Lopes da Silva represents the generation that was motivated by the land struggle, evictions, and violence against the seringueiros. Ivanilde Lopes da Silva found in her leadership role in the base communities the inspiration to involve herself in bold mobilization efforts, and to model a liberating form of education as a rural teacher. Her own experience with schooling had been a traumatic one of failure and fear of a hostile teacher. Though Ivanilde Lopes da Silva has not been part of Projeto Seringueiro per se, her work in the social movement and in rural education dovetails with that of Projeto Seringueiro, and her experiences illustrate important ways in which the objectives of Projeto Seringueiro have become institutionalized in rural education in Acre.

Francisca "Chiquinha" da Silva represents the next generation, whose parents suffered the hardships of eviction, loss of livelihood, and migration to the city during the land struggle of the 1970s. Her early experience with education couldn't be more different than Ivanilde Lopes da Silva's, for instead of blows from an irate teacher, she received encouragement from her mother who had herself been the scribe for her seringal before it was sold to ranchers from the South. Chiquinha da Silva views the Projeto Seringueiro generation as a model to emulate,

109

and she strives to keep the flame alive during a time with values often inimical to those that animated Projeto Seringueiro's founders and leaders. Chiquinha da Silva's voice conveys the frustrations that accompany institutionalization and the move from a civil-society NGO to a state bureaucracy.

Manoel Estébio Cavalcante da Cunha's account spans both Ivanilde Lopes da Silva's and Chiquinha da Silva's generations, covering the entire period of Projeto Seringueiro's existence. Thus, his story offers the most complete narrative of Project Rubber Tapper's history and of the ideas that motivated it from its inception. So closely identified are CTA/Projeto Seringueiro's history and da Cunha's own biography that his evolution from seminarian to community organizer to educator, and from the nongovernmental to the state sector, describe the journey of Projeto Seringueiro itself from alternative to mainstream. Da Cunha, one of Projeto Seringueiro's four original teachers, is currently working in indigenous education, where he draws heavily on his Projeto Seringueiro experience.

In these interviews, we see once again the interrelated influences of Freire's pedagogy, liberation theology, Marxism, and a powerful environmental consciousness that becomes more important by the day as new challenges threaten the Amazon.

Ivanilde Lopes da Silva

I have not been part of Projeto Seringueiro, but I have worked in a parallel fashion in rural education for many years, sharing the same goals,

Photo by author.

Ivanilde Lopes da Silva

problems, and motivations as Projeto Seringueiro. The best place to start is with my childhood in the seringal, because it has influenced all my choices since then. As a child, I lived very close to nature, and though we experienced many hardships, it is comforting to recall that closeness today in the city.

When I was born, I already had four older siblings, but they all died of "childhood illness," they called it. My parents lived in Alto Purús, in the seringal Maracajú, but conditions were harsh and my father left for Boca do Acre, a one-month journey by canoe, hoping to find a better life for us in Acre where there was more rubber; that would've been about the mid-1940s. However, what awaited us in seringal Glória was more poverty. My father made the first clearing there and built a makeshift house with a straw roof for us. Then other families began to arrive, living in the same house with us, and I remember very well sitting on the floor listening to them relate their adventures and hardships. Things didn't turn out as my father had hoped when he first came from the Northeast eager to make a new start, with no skills save a second-grade education and the ability to recite *cordel* literature—folk stories in verse—which he knew by heart.

My most vivid memory, however, was not of stories, but of the huge, resplendent riverboats that would come down the river. We would hear the piercing whistle an hour before the boat would arrive because of all the curves, and we would all be there on the riverbank waiting for it to round the bend. The *banzeiro,* the 20-meter wake the boat makes, would drench the clothes drying on the riverbank and swamp the canoes. It was a big event for us. Our house was on the high riverbank, and if it was night, we would compete to be the first to spy the big spotlights of the boat. The river was the center of our life. We children would play at the water's edge, fish, carry water on our heads. We would bring Brazil nuts, seringueira fruit, coconut, and bananas to the water, and we would bathe in the river, which was very clean.

My first day of school in Catuaba was not a pleasant memory, and perhaps it will give you an idea of what schooling—if you could call it that, when it existed—was like in the seringal in the 1950s. First, I had a hard time understanding my teacher's accent, so I could never really know what she was saying about math or the alphabet. The main problem was that when you made a mistake, she would hit your hand with a ruler or make you kneel on corn meal, so I was always very tense and couldn't concentrate. I remember going by canoe to class with my brothers and sisters, who also were afraid of the teacher. The classroom was an alien place for me. My biggest fear was that I would get ruler blows to the head if I didn't know the answers, because the teacher had beaten my friend so hard that she had broken the ruler. At that time, you had to go up and stand in front of the teacher and recite the lesson. The closer I got to the teacher, the louder I would cry. Needless to say, I didn't learn anything.

My father spent all year gathering rubber and *sernambí,* that is, the leavings, which he would load into his canoe to sell in the city. Actually, he would steal it because seringueiros were not allowed to buy or sell anything; all purchases had to be made through the company store, and money was never used since all the seringueiros' purchases were recorded as debts. My father would sell *sernambí* whenever he needed money for our school clothes; he also made my rubber shoes, rubber balls for me to take to school, and rubber for the drum to play the national anthem on Independence Day. We were extremely poor; we were able to go to school because our colocação was near the headquarters where the patrão lived.

The riverboats came replete with wonderful things. First, they carried beautiful sailors dressed all in white; they were a dazzling sight. Second, they brought supplies like oil and farinha, which we would watch them unload, after which they would load the Brazil nuts and rubber to take to the city. Various convoys of about 15 burros each would arrive from the interior of the seringal carrying rubber for the boat. They would unload their cargo and seringueiros, burros, everyone, would all bathe in the river. Afterward, they would load up the burros with the newly arrived supplies and head back into the forest. They would leave about a kilometer of rubber *pelles,* large balls of smoked rubber, lined up all along the riverbank waiting to be loaded on the ship, and we would jump and play on them trying not to get our feet caught between the hard, 50-pound balls.

Everything took place at the headquarters on the river; it was like a great show. You could see it all from the large veranda of the building. Many weddings took place there. I remember there were lots of lights; it looked like a lovely city. I always wanted to run errands, like buying the kerosene, in order to see what was happening at the big house and the store. I remember one particularly beautiful wedding in the seringal. The judge had been sent for by the patrão to celebrate the seringalista's daughter's wedding. We watched her wedding, amazed at all the starched petticoats and shirts and dresses, and I was like starch, sticking to everything, including the dancing. Until I was about 11 years old I would attend all the parties. We would dance the *forró* to the accompaniment of accordion, tambourine, and triangle. Lighted *porongas* would be placed all around to illuminate the room; it was a memorable sight. After I was

11 I had to stay at home and learn the domestic arts because that was the custom at the time. Even so, I enjoyed great freedom and happiness as a child and lived very close to nature and in unity with my family in the seringal.

When I got married I had no money for a bridal dress or anything else. We simply went to Porto Acre because that's where the nearest judge lived, and where Zé, my husband, was working. Though Zé was a teacher, he was working as the recorder/cashier of the seringal, and I taught in his place. But first I needed preparation because I had stopped my own studies after the second year. My brother-in-law, who was a teacher in Catu-aba where we live, gave me special tutoring so I could complete third and fourth grade, take the test, and become certified.

Thank heavens my brother-in-law prepared me intensively because I could barely sign my name, and the third-grade teacher whom I had begun with had herself only gone to the third grade. So my base was very weak, to say the least. Zé also helped me a great deal because he had completed the first through fourth grades without interruption, knew how to prepare plans, and was an experienced teacher. Later, I became a fourth-grade teacher through Mobral, the government's accelerated literacy program begun by Paulo Freire. My first salary ever was from Mobral. I had never received anything for my previous eight years of teaching, but that was the norm then. This was in 1975, well before Projeto Seringueiro, and you can see the desperate need for education for the seringueiros, quite apart from the question of the land struggle.

In 1974 I began my work with the base communities. I was called by Dom Moacyr, who was celebrating Mass on the radio and spoke of the gospel lesson of the table is large but the servers are few. I was fixing breakfast, the children were crying, there was noise and confusion in our household, and I turned on the radio. It was as if Dom Moacyr were speaking to me personally. He said in his homily, "There in the seringais, on the riverbanks, there is someone who would like to do evangelization. Come, look for us, God is calling you." That touched me profoundly, and I stood there crying in the kitchen. I wanted to change my life, catechize, and this was my call. My mother-in-law came to visit every Sunday for lunch. When she got off the boat, I started crying and told her that I wanted to form a catechist group. We talked about it over lunch, and she was extremely supportive, saying, "God is calling you." Though I was six months pregnant, I left to stand for hours in the hot sun at the bishop's residence. There was a long line of poor people, many of whom were ill and had been carried from the interior in their hammocks and mosquito netting to request a favor or to receive a last blessing. Finally my turn came, and I was ushered into the bishop's study where I told my story. Dom Moacyr gave me a Bible and two catechist books and said, "It was God who sent you. You will learn by doing, evangelizing yourself by evangelizing others." That's when I began a new chapter in my life.

I returned home, attended an adult training session directed by Padre José Migaña in December, and had my baby in January. My group's first Mass was held May 1, 1975, outdoors under the trees beside my house. We had three marriages, 40 baptisms, and Dom Moacyr himself gave a beautiful homily there in Catuaba on the riverbank. He spoke in terms of sowing good seed, that seeds sown on riverbanks will grow, and that I had a responsibility to nurture them. He sent Padre Otávio Deustro to talk with me, a very animated, activist priest, who then involved me in his work. As a result, our one small group multiplied in five years to eight large evangelization groups on the riverbank. Then I went to Imaculada Conceição church, where I worked in evangelization for 16 years.

This was all within the context of the fight for the land, and liberation theology was our strength and inspiration in the base communities. In the schools there were similar beliefs expressed; certainly there was the view that education cannot be closed off from the world, that it has to be open, involved, have a social vision. To be Christian meant to be involved in the problems of your community. Many teachers in Projeto Seringueiro were inspired by the base communities or were themselves catechists. During the social movement, everyone—Projeto Seringueiro leaders, union workers, base community groups—were all reading, talking, studying, and broadening our knowledge of our situation and the world. It was a fantastic experience, and I was deeply engaged in the movement of the eighties through my work at Immaculate Conception. It was extremely difficult, but it was exhilarating! For example, I took a course in social analysis at Imaculada with Nilson Mourão, who later became state senator. He gave us many readings about development and multinationals in an excellent course that showed me the light. After that, I fought vigorously for the union, the school, and the rights of the seringueiros, both those in the forest and those displaced to the city.

In the forest I was the principal coordinator of all the base communities involved in the empates in Catuaba where we were trying to save our seringal, first from the ranchers who came in the early 1970s, and then from INCRA, the land reform agency. Yes, this was one of the first empates; we had to meet secretly at night or we would have been beaten and arrested. We would meet and read the Bible and talk about what was happening to us, and try to determine how to face this challenge as Christians; the empate was definitely the correct way. We would face down those who were cutting the trees and not leave. It was terrible to see them cutting down the magnificent rubber and Brazil nut trees as if they were nothing, to make way for cattle. We would camp out in the forest, and they would have to drag us away.

We continued after INCRA took over the property and began parceling out plots to seringueiros. I directed three sit-ins at the office of the superintendent of INCRA, fighting for our right to the land, a decent school, a health post, and a dirt access road. Zé and I were elementary teachers at the state school there in Catuaba, which was falling to pieces; it was a disgrace. No one even wanted to enter it, and we had to fight constantly for every single thing. Being a teacher meant being completely involved as a leader in defending your community. INCRA did divide up the seringal, but we were finally given some land and our other rights, including a new school, but that didn't come about until Jorge Viana became governor. The empates at seringal Catuaba are very well known. My oldest daughter teaches there today, and she is working to preserve the whole story through my oral history.

In the base communities we talked a lot about turning the tables. The objective was to turn the table without breaking it, to find viable, peaceful alternatives. Everyone in the base communities was reading the leading theologians as well as Che, who was a heroic figure to all of us. It was a time of intellectual, religious, and social agitation as we defended the seringueiro and the land.

In the city I was very involved as one of the earliest organizers of the social movement. I have founded so many associations that I cannot remember them all. For example, in Rio Branco I was a founder of the Chico Mendes school of CUT, the Workers Central Union; the school is a leadership training school, and now there are a number of them throughout the state. I founded the Association of Sick Persons in Rio Branco and Goiana for indigent people who were not being treated at all, and I organized a volunteer intercity bus service to pick these people up and help them get free medical attention. I also founded the Association of Working Men and Women to help them present their case for a minimum wage. The working poor had long been neglected because they had no organization, but after a while they won the minimum wage and Acre was a national leader in setting a minimum wage. I started the Acre Women's Network to advocate for pay for rural agricultural and urban domestic workers who could not live on what they were making. We also gave numerous workshops to help these women build their self-esteem. They had been treated as nothing for so long that they began to believe they were worthless. I must say, those workshops were wonderful for me, too—so reaffirming. We also worked hard to address the issue of domestic violence in many workshops. I organized caravans of buses to go to Brasília to advocate for these groups as part of a national effort, and I gave speeches to national gatherings not only in Brasília but also in Rio and São Paulo on behalf of the poor, either before government or base community assemblies. The organization that I began that is closest to my heart is the one I spent so many years directing, the Teachers Union in Rio Branco, for teachers of first through third grade. That union has brought many improvements to another group that had previously been completely ignored.

Of course, if the PT hadn't eventually come into office, we never would have achieved all that we have here in Acre. We were part of a network of unions, neighborhood associations, organizations at the local, municipal, and state levels—all working for change from dictatorship to democracy. And when one of us, Lula, from a poor northeastern background, was elected president, we were overjoyed. There are now many programs to help the poor, the infirm, and the hungry. Did you know that Lula and Chico were good friends? Yes, and Lula used to come often to Xapuri and ride on horseback in the seringais with Chico. He knows Xapuri like the back of his hand.

Returning to my educational biography, the other turning point in my life, besides the call to evangelization, occurred in 1977 when my brother-in-law died. Not only had he tutored me, he also encouraged me to enroll in a supplementary program for rural teachers. I studied weekends and holidays in that program while also teaching first and second grades. Zé was teaching third and fourth, and we had eight children, so it was quite difficult for the three years it took to complete the basic education program—that is, through eighth grade. After that, I went on to complete secondary school in teaching. Zé didn't want me to continue—he was a bit machista in that—but finally he agreed, and then, seeing that it was a good idea, he enrolled, too.

When I began working at Ensino Rural in 1999 when Binho Marques became secretary of education and Jorge Viana became governor, I became part of the rural education team. My job has been primarily to *conscientizar* the communities—that is, prepare them for how to accept, treat, and appreciate schools, how to take pride in education and value it. Rural communities did not have this tradition, and the state schools that existed were not worthy of the name. They were falling down, had no teaching materials; often teachers would not show up, or were incompetent, so no one respected them or the idea of education. There would be arguments between the teachers and the communities, because many times the teachers just wanted the salary and did not care about teaching. So there was so much to overcome, a whole history of bad experiences. That's where my community organizing and communication skills and nearly 30 years of experience came in handy. I love the seringal and I know all the families, as well as the paths and small rivers in the area. I visited everyone in neighboring communities many times, listening to their complaints and telling them that things would now be different, but that they have to help assume the responsibility of having and caring for the schools. Another part of my job was to get the environmental message across to them, that they have to take care of the forest and the local rivers, which are endangered. I also helped communities resolve disputes, so my responsibilities have been more practical than technical. I worked nonstop for over four years, sometimes rowing seven hours and walking three hours in a day, but my sciatica became much worse, and I can no longer travel the rivers, which I love so much; however, I can still journey by car and on foot.

I would like to make one important observation from my perspective in the Office of Rural Education: Projeto Seringueiro had a tremendous influence on rural education. What happened is that communities would see technicians arriving in the seringal, all that activity, and neighbors and teachers building schools, the whole community becoming involved. And all of this was for rubber tappers and their children who had never before had anything at all, and people in rural communities, such as the ones where I worked, began to see that those children in the forest were learning. Then the children of agricultural families and the parents themselves began to think that if education could work for the seringueiros, then maybe it could for them, too. Projeto Seringueiro had a huge effect; it was a great motivation and example for all other rural communities.

When I think back, remembering how I started out, traumatized by my school experience in the seringal, having failed the first-grade exams three times, and acutely embarrassed about my shabby appearance next to the other children taking the exams, I would have never dreamed that I would ever become a teacher. Nor would I have imagined that I would play a leadership role in the base communities, or help found unions and women's groups, or coordinate intercity political activities on behalf of the poor, all of which require the ability to read, write, and interpret written materials. Just as we do not know what the future will bring us, neither do we know what we are capable of achieving until we are faced with new challenges.

Francisca "Chiquinha" das Chagas Souza da Silva

When I was a young child in the seringal, I had a strong desire to learn to read and write in order to be able to teach these skills to other serin-

Photo by author.

Francisca "Chiquinha" das Chagas Souza da Silva

gueiros. Where we lived only my mother knew how to read and write; neither my father nor anyone else in the seringal had any schooling. My mother knew because she was the daughter and granddaughter of the owners of the seringal. Actually the family was heavily in debt; with the collapse of rubber prices they lost everything and were forced to sell out to the ranchers in 1973 for practically nothing. But before that my mother had received some education in Boca do Acre in the municipality of Amazonas. When she returned home for school vacation, she met my father, fell in love with him, married, and left school. But she had learned to read, write, and do the four math operations. After that, she was the scribe in the seringal, writing letters for everyone and reading for them the letters they received. She taught my older sisters to read and write from an old book of ABCs that she herself had used. To teach the alphabet, she would scratch the letters in the dirt, cover each one with a small piece of paper, and ask the students to remember and identify what was underneath. I would come close and try to join in, but I was very young, and my mother would say, "Don't worry, your turn will come."

I was born in 1967 and was seven years old when we left the seringal for Rio Branco, saying good-bye to the colocação São Joaquim and the Antimari River. Because the seringal had been sold, everyone had to leave and find a new way to make a living. My father wanted to move to another seringal in another region, but my mother said that would just be the same story, and the only alternative was to try life in the city and put the children in school. My father saw no reason for us to learn to read and write, but my mother insisted. So they sold their utensils for making farinha and came to the city, against my father's wishes. Unfortunately the boat we took ran into an embankment at night when it was pitch black, overturned, and we lost everything, all our clothes and our chickens.

We arrived in Rio Branco with no money, no possessions, and no place to live. We finally found a makeshift shelter with a palm roof, next to a farm in a remote area of the São Francisco neighborhood. My maternal grandfather had just enough from the sale of the seringal to purchase a very small piece of land near the road to Porto do Acre, so we moved there.

I began school at age eight, in 1975. My mother had a hard time keeping us in school because we were so many children. My father did not have a profession; he only knew how to tap rubber and plant crops. He tried his hand at everything you can imagine in the city—mechanic's assistant, construction worker's assistant—but it was not enough to live on. So my mother had to find work—weeding people's vegetable gardens, washing clothes; it was very difficult. We also went out to work at a very young age in order to help my parents. I started babysitting at age nine; then my mother and I went to work as domestic servants. As time went on, my father saw that it wasn't working out staying there in the city with all 12 children, so he took the younger ones to live with him on a small plot of land in a resettlement program sponsored by INCRA, the land reform agency.

The good news in all this is that, in spite of all the material difficulties—whether by luck, illumination, divine protection, whatever—we all stayed very close, and my mother and father were devoted parents who always conducted us along an extremely ethical path, giving us a consistent and very strong morality.

My paternal grandmother also played an important role in our formation, especially our religious instruction. My grandparents arrived here from Ceará in the 1940s, attracted by the Vargas government's wartime recruiting program for "rubber soldiers," and eager to escape the drought in the Northeast. It was only after she passed away that I realized how much I had learned from her; in particular, I learned about ethics. I later read about ethics in philosophy books, and I studied it at the university, but it seemed so abstract until I realized that this is what my grandmother practiced every day. She taught us the Golden Rule, "Do unto others as you would have them do unto you." Sometimes a beggar would come by—there were always people poorer than we were—who would tell us a sad story, and my grandmother would help him out. She taught us always to give, even if it is only a glass of water.

My grandmother was also very religious. Where we lived there was no church, but we had a service at home every evening at six. After we had our baths we would kneel down in front of the saints, and my grandmother would light a candle and turn on the radio. We would hear the Ave Maria and then pray the prayers that my grandmother had taught us. It is a beautiful memory, and today, though I practice Kardeckian spiritism, I still keep the practice of taking a moment each day to give thanks for the blessings of life.

My mother, father, and my grandmother were all people of strong moral character. It is quite an accomplishment that all the children have had the opportunity to become educated; this was my mother's objective in life. We older ones, as we studied and began working, would help the younger ones go to school.

After I finished the first eight years of school, the basic cycle, I wanted to continue studying in order to become an agricultural technician and later an agronomist so I could help the seringueiros with food production for their families. I wanted to work in rural extension because my father had that plot I mentioned, and I could see the anguish of the former seringueiros struggling to survive, because I helped him out there as another worker, and experienced the land issue firsthand with my father.

The problem was that the only school with an agricultural program here in Acre was for internal students, and they accepted only male applicants. This was in the 1980s, and the discrimination of machismo was still very strong. That's why I was unable to go on in agronomy. So what did I do? First I cried because my family could not afford to pay for any of the technical programs that were offered at the secondary level. Of course that was useless, so I set about finding a program that was affordable and would enable me to support myself in the city. I decided by elimination—accounting, administration, nurse technician—until only teaching was left. My first two years studying education were very difficult because I was still not committed to pedagogy. Though as a child I had wanted to teach in the seringal, by the time I was a late adolescent I not only wanted to become an agronomist, I had also convinced myself that I would not be a good teacher; I completely lacked confidence in my abilities. Fortunately, in my third year of teacher preparation, my mentor Marília Sant'Ana offered me the opportunity to teach in a brand-new elementary school, so I gave it a try, enjoyed it, and at the end of the year (this was in 1986), the director of the school asked me to take charge of a literacy program at the Colégio da Aplicação the following year. This was a big vote of confidence, but still, I kept thinking, *I'm no good at this. Soon they are going to find out and be so disappointed.*

Then I began looking back on my childhood, and my mother reminded me that in the seringal I had wanted to be a teacher, and that here in the city my first teacher was impressed that I had learned to read and write almost immediately on starting school. Now I see clearly the influence of my mother and the early images I have of her teaching other people. Unlike other children either in the seringal or the poor districts

122 Schools in the Forest

of the city, my first contact with reading was at home, not at school, so
the world of reading and writing was a familiar universe for me. I also
reflected on how, as soon as I arrived in the city and entered school, I was
always making scribblings on scraps of paper to mail to my godmother
back in the seringal. Later, when I was nine years old and had learned to
read and write, every afternoon my mother would put up an old piece
of plywood on the wall outside our house. The neighbor children would
come over, and I would give them classes. I gathered empty oil cans to
make the legs of the desk and put a board across them for the top. I
would bring out the pieces of chalk my mother had carefully guarded,
and we would have class.

When my self-confidence was low and I was having doubts about
my ability as a teacher, my mother helped me recall all of this as well as
my earliest desire to teach in the forest. In effect, that is precisely what I
have done as an adult, in that I have dedicated myself to rural education.
I had wanted to become a technical agronomist because hunger is widespread, but in either case, all my desires and projects, consciously and un-
consciously, have been directed to the rural population.

Like other seringueiros, I come from an oral tradition, that of the
seringal, but unlike others, I have the additional heritage of the written
word because of my mother. I realize that it is unusual to have a foot in
each world, the oral and the lettered, and I feel very strongly the responsibility to use the latter to be of service to the seringueiro.

After I had passed my competitive exam and taught basic literacy at
the Colégio da Aplicação for a year, I was invited to work as a teacher in
a literacy program for the university maintenance, security, and food
service staff of the Universidade Federal do Acre (UFAC), who were almost all illiterate. At that time they did not have to pass any exam in
order to be hired; they were just named by politicians, so they did not
necessarily have job skills or any education. This was in 1986. I still hadn't
graduated yet, but since they needed a substitute teacher, I took the job,
as usual doubting that I could do it, and hoping that no one would discover my incompetence.

The team at UFAC produced their own materials, very closely related to the liberating pedagogical principles of Paulo Freire. I worked with
generative terms and problem posing, all of which was very Freireian and

a fabulous experience for me. I also learned more about the university's extension programs and was able to create some of the materials they began using in the extensions in the interior of Acre.

At the end of the 1980s I took more exams given by the municipality of Rio Branco in order to become officially certified to teach the first through fourth levels of basic education. I also received my degree in pedagogy from UFAC. Then I was invited to give literacy classes to poor women in a very marginal neighborhood, a prostitution zone.

The neighborhood was called Bairro do Papoco. The work there was begun by the Sisters of the Instituição São José. The church had a parish center there where the Sisters would open two classrooms in the evening for the prostitutes. The municipal secretary's office didn't want me to go there because it was very dangerous, and up until then they had hired only male teachers. However, I eagerly took the job as a way to be of service, and taught there for two years. Whenever students would fail to appear in class, I would go up and down the riverbanks searching for them, telling them how important it was to attend and urging them to return. Usually they did. Before long the personnel at the municipal secretary's office began to find my work interesting, and they called me to help a team of young people write teaching materials for students in literacy classes. When I told them that I didn't have any idea how to write materials, they laughed and encouraged me, so I became part of that team. I still have a copy of the resulting text at home: "The Road of Learning," it was called.

In these comings and going in the beginning of the 1990s when Jorge Viana assumed the mayor's office, and Binho Marques became municipal secretary of education, I was invited to form part of the technical team of the secretary of education's office responsible for the early elementary years. I had graduated by then, and I came on board in education.

That was when I met Pingo Ferreira. I had seen him earlier speaking at large events as one of the main pillars of education in the state, but we didn't begin working together until 1993 when he asked me to offer suggestions for the *Poronga* student workbook that he was writing for Projeto Seringueiro.

In 1991, right after my graduation, a professor of mine had helped make it possible for me to receive a scholarship to do graduate study at the University of Campinas in São Paulo, but I was very timid, and my family's finances were precarious, so I did not feel that I could leave my brothers and sisters without my assistance. Everything has its own time, and it was not time to leave. So I worked for three years on the technical team for Binho Marques, the municipal secretary of education. Then I moved to João Pessoa to attend the Universidade Federal da Paraíba, where they had a master's program in popular education for youth and adults, my area of interest and expertise. Professor Timothy Denis Ireland, who is British, was my supervisor as well as the coordinator of both the program and international relations for the university.

I had hoped to do my master's on the remarkable achievements of the Projeto Seringueiro educational team a decade earlier in literacy, organizing the seringueiros, and in working with the union. I wanted very much to record the dramatic experience that changed so many lives nearly a generation ago. I had already begun to document Projeto Seringueiro's history and had conducted some interviews, including one with Pingo Ferreira that I had a hard time transcribing, not only because he speaks rapid fire, but also because he has his own unique way of expressing himself, almost a language all his own. I was interested in Projeto Seringueiro's teacher training and wanted to relate it to the actual classroom situation in order to see how the workshop ideas and materials were applied in practice.

However, my supervisor said that was too much, that I had only two years to complete everything, and that I needed to reduce the scope of my plan drastically. Since I was always talking about Projeto Seringueiro's pedagogical materials, he suggested that I focus on one aspect—the use of technologies in Projeto Seringueiro—which would be manageable in the allotted time. That became my focus, even though it turned out that the use of instructional technologies was not a major factor in the formation of Projeto Seringueiro's teachers.

When I finished the master's, I thought I would work for five years and then go on for the doctorate, but I no longer want to do that. The first reason is that I absolutely love working in basic education with Manoel Estébio da Cunha and Pingo Ferreira. I have learned so much from them that it is like continuing my graduate education. Second, I absolutely love going into the forest; it is like going home for me. Levi-Strauss is correct when he says that when you are a researcher you also are a subject; you enter into your work. It is very hard—I think it is impossible, actually—

to exempt oneself from the study, but one has to try if one is ever going to write anything. The most difficult thing for me was to exempt myself, at least somewhat, systematize my research, and then write. That experience again reminded me that I am more from an oral than a written culture, because I never really believed that I could write a thesis, but I did it, with Professor Timothy's encouragement.

Writing my thesis helped me see clearly that the work that we did in Projeto Seringueiro has now become public policy. This is quite amazing, because it was not very long ago that two things were true: First, that Projeto Seringueiro and the whole social movement of which it was a part had absolutely no political power; on the contrary, all the cards were stacked against their success. Second, anyone from the city, and that includes even very small towns like Xapuri, was viewed by the seringueiro as a threat, someone who was likely to throw them off their land, burn their house and the forest. For these reasons it is truly remarkable that the movement that Projeto Seringueiro and the CTA helped build grew strong enough to force the state to assume its proper role regarding the right to education and to make rural education public policy. When we won the government—that is, when Jorge Viana became governor and Binho Marques, secretary of education—I left the NGO sector that CTA/Projeto Seringueiro represented and began working for the state. Manoel Estébio da Cunha left to work with the indigenous, and I, with the rural populations.

When I returned from Paraíba with my master's degree in September 1998, Jorge's election campaign for governor was in full swing. I took part in the campaign and also worked at CTA/Projeto Seringueiro. At that time Binho Marques was president of the CTA, and he asked me, Manoel da Cunha, Pingo Ferreira, and a few others to formalize the pedagogical project of the CTA, because, while they had accomplished a great deal, they had practically no written records. We got as far as making an outline of Projeto Seringueiro's trajectory, but we didn't get any further because Jorge called Binho to become secretary of education; then Binho in 1998 called Manoel and me to be part of his team. In January 1999 we began, which means that almost the entire technical team of the CTA/Projeto Seringueiro left to work for the government, leaving the CTA with practically no staff and Pingo virtually by himself in Projeto Seringueiro.

In the Office of Rural Education today, I still see some continuity with Projeto Seringueiro in terms of ideals and social and intellectual inspiration, but I am reminded in my work every single day that we are now living in a very different world. Particularly in the 1980s, our principal objective was to guarantee everyone the basic right to education, especially the seringueiros and forest populations who had never had any rights. We hoped also to continue with that same enthusiasm and dynamism of the earlier years. I think that it is still possible, but it is very difficult. Institutionalization has its own problems, and they are different from the ones we faced earlier.

For one thing I work with small groups in different communities, and as their numbers have multiplied, my challenges have multiplied along with them, so that's an issue of scale. The other, more serious challenge is that the government of Acre consists of many disparate components. It's not just one political party or one point of view, but many—not just people who see things the way we do in the education team but numerous groups whose values and interests are often completely opposed to ours. I would even go so far as to say that it is more difficult to work with these groups than it is to guarantee that a school be built and supplied with teachers and materials in the most remote part of the state.

We have meetings together, discuss issues, but make little headway; the very composition of our teams makes progress unlikely. We have a strategic plan, we know where we would like to go and how to get there, we are very organized, but it is virtually impossible to get any decision through this obstructionist group that is really not interested in education. On bad days I would say that such people constitute the majority of those I have to work with, and I often feel as if I am rowing against a strong current that threatens to swamp the boat.

My father used to say that the number of shameless scoundrels just keeps growing, and I'm afraid I often feel that he is correct, that the negative is often stronger than the positive. That's why I have to hold on to the ethics and values I learned from my family. It's either that or just give up. I'm talking specifically about the difficulty of working with opportunistic people who care nothing for truth and just want personal advantage; they know and care nothing about education or about the poor. What they want is power—power to put into practice their own pet projects, their party's projects—and to benefit personally. When people advance their own personal agendas, very ugly things happen. When you call them on it, they act like they don't know what you are talking about. This is a big challenge for me every day.

Binho Marques is very determined to serve the public, and he fights such interests; he negotiates a bit with them but not much. Jorge was more, "What do you want? I'll give it to you and then you go away." Democracy is still a bit new in Brazil, and there are many disappointments as we have moved from one extreme to the other—from not having any democracy to thinking that we can do everything.

By and large, I would have to say that the successors of Projeto Seringueiro do not have the same capacity for commitment to social ideals that the earlier generation did. True, there is still a small group, but I don't see how they can continue that dedication because the influence of those who are extremely individualistic is much stronger today than that of those who are community minded. It is also true that we have been so involved in securing our social objectives that, not only have we not put things in writing, we have not prepared successors either, so there is no new generation of leaders. I am referring not only to CTA/Projeto Seringueiro, but also to the PT and the Communist Party, whose leadership is very poorly prepared and very immature in comparison with that of our generation.

Our political, social, and historical moment was very different; we were moved by the urgent need to organize or be completely overrun, destroyed. I have told you so much about my family because, for many of us, our parents were our greatest influence; we were brought up to have tremendous respect for them. That is why we will never forget seeing them disrespected. The inhuman dispossession of their land, what terrible disrespect! That experience was emblazoned in our consciousness and motivated us to mobilize in a collective response that was both political and educational as we fought for basic rights for the poor. Environmentalism was also a large part of Projeto Seringueiro, and even before Chico Mendes there were very active environmentalists. For example, Ivanilde and Padre Alberto Morini galvanized resistance to the invasion of the ranchers from the South, and worked tirelessly to protect the forest. Ivanilde was not part of Projeto Seringueiro, but she was an influential teacher and an amazing mobilizer in the seringais and in the city slums for many years. She is perhaps best known for her leadership in the base communities

worked for the environment and for education for the
ople have had a page in this important story. Chico's
ttention to the environmental issues that local leaders
for some time, and that were an intrinsic part of Projeto
Seringueiro's mission and identity.

My goal is to continue to add to the story. My deepest desire is to
formulate and implement a rural educational policy that would offer
everyone the kind of education that enables them to think about themselves and the world around them, and not permit other people to think
or do for them. This is the legacy of Projeto Seringueiro, and, despite the
entrenched and unprincipled special-interest groups, I am determined
because once you start down this road, you can't turn back. Once you
open your eyes, you're never going to close them again. Many communities have schools now, and some are quite good. My satisfaction comes
from working for the whole community, the common good, perhaps because I come from a big family in which we had to multiply the little we
had; circumstances obliged us always to think about the other. I would
like to have a guarantee that things would continue to improve, and that
entrenched interests would not prevail, but there are no guarantees in
this world. In the meantime, I am working to strengthen my spiritual-
ity; knowing that I can be of service to others helps a great deal.

Manoel Estébio Cavalcante da Cunha

I was a seminarian in the northeastern state of Ceará in 1980 when Padre
Heitor Turrini came from Acre to give a vocational talk at our seminary.

Photo by author.

Manoel Estébio
Cavalcante da Cunha

He introduced us to a completely different
world from that of the desert Northeast. I
was captivated by the stories he told of Acre,
the film he showed of the lush exuberance of
Amazônia, and the history of struggle of the
people, first to become a territory and a state,
and then the current struggle to defend their
right to their land. So I made the journey to
Acre and spent my first year in Rio Branco as
a novitiate with the Servants of Mary. In 1981
I moved to Xapuri to help advise the union

(STR) because Padre Cláudio Deustro, the parish priest for Xapuri, was also head of the CDT (Commission in Defense of the Worker) in Acre and traveled a lot, so I was the one responsible in his absence.

That was about the time that Projeto Seringueiro was born. When Mary Allegretti, Ronaldo Lima de Oliveira, and others would come to Xapuri they would stay at the parish house and have their meals there en route to the seringal. I remember when the first version of *Poronga* was made, Mary gave a copy to Bishop Dom Moacyr, which he passed on to me and another seminarian, Paulo Klein, asking us to give it a critical reading. Klein taught nursing at the university, and he was creating a similar text, but it was very simple and handmade, because he was doing this on his own and as part of his internship in the seringal, where he saw how great the need was for education. Dom Moacyr shared *Poronga* with us when he made a pastoral visit to Xapuri and we accompanied him to seringal Equador.

The parish house in Xapuri was a gathering place for those involved in the social movement, and it was there that I met Dercy Teles and fell in love with her practically at first sight. She was a pastoral agent and syndicate leader at the time. She soon became the first woman president of the union (STR) in the entire Amazon region. Shortly after we got married, we were invited to form part of the very first team of teachers for Projeto Seringueiro in 1982.

We moved to colocação Já com Fome (Already Hungry) in seringal Nazaré, along with Ronaldo and his wife Marlete. The four of us lived there from 1982 to 1984, working with literacy, health, union advising—with associativism, that is, with the cooperative—and we were assisted by Oxfam in the purchase of merchandise, so that seringueiros would not have to sell to the middlemen; CESE, another NGO, helped, too. The school in Já com Fome drew students from Nazaré, which was a very large seringal; from São Pedro, another large seringal; and seringal Tupac, which was smaller.

The school was very closely tied to the union, and when Dercy decided that she wanted to leave office, having gotten the union through a difficult transition period in terms of leadership, she decided to do another kind of work. So Ronaldo ran for election but lost, which was a very good thing because we discovered that, however great our commitment,

)t rural workers ourselves. Soon other communities associated
syndicate asked us to start schools, and it became clear we
replicate the unique experience in Já com Fôme because we
were the only teachers, and there was simply no one living in the seringal who was prepared to teach.

So we asked for funds from the MEC (Ministry of Education and
Culture) and Oxfam, and, using Freire's methodology, mounted an intensive course to prepare rubber tappers to teach in their own communities. Ronaldo, Marlete, Dercy, and I, who had been the teachers, then
moved on to teacher education in 1983. That was also the year that the
CTA was created. Mary Allegretti was crucial in that process, and the
new people who began entering CTA/Projeto Seringueiro also worked in
the teacher training course. That was when Projeto Seringueiro expanded
from the one school there in Nazaré in Já com Fome.

Remember that the schools were linked to a larger project, the land
question, because the great challenge at that time was to find a way to
allow the seringueiros to remain in the forest. The only alternative that
the authorities were offering were projects to convert the seringais into
agricultural modules, but the seringueiros only had experience with subsistence agriculture. Those who ventured out to try these settlement projects were unable to support their families because they could not produce
extensively. Not to mention that at that time, even though Acre was isolated, agricultural products cheaper than those produced in Acre began
arriving here from the outside, the result of economic globalization. Rice
and beans were much cheaper; seringueiros had no way of competing
with these prices, nor did they know how to farm extensively. Another
problem was that the lots were too small. Some of us tried to convince
INCRA, the Agrarian Reform Agency, to increase the allotment from
the inadequate 25 to 75 hectares to a more reasonable 150, but the fact
is that what INCRA really wanted was to throw the seringueiro off the
land so that it would be available for the large cattle ranchers who had
arrived here beginning in the 1970s.

The land problem was critical; this is one reason that the National
Encounter of Rubber Tappers in 1985 in Brasília was a milestone for the
rubber tappers' movement. Dercy Teles, Armando Soares Filho, Fátima,
and Ronaldo Lima de Oliveira from the CTA/Projeto Seringueiro team

worked on it; Ronaldo helped obtain financing from Oxfam; and Mary Allegretti and Marlete Lima de Oliveira did a tremendous amount of organizing in Brasília. The Encontro owed much to Mary's efforts; the role she played in Brasília making contacts was absolutely crucial. We also made contacts in Amazônia, Rondônia, and Pará, but the planning was based here in Acre; the idea came from here, and the idea for the extractive reserves was first thought out here in Acre. The Encontro was an attempt to come out of isolation because the problems in Acre were the same for all seringueiros of the Amazon, but there was no forum for discussing the situation. Then, the National Council of Rubber Tappers (Conselho Nacional de Seringueiros) was created by myself and others; the Encontro took place in September; and during that entire year I worked hard in mobilization. Projeto Seringueiro's teachers played a very important role at the Encontro. They participated actively, made critiques during discussions, helped produce the proposal for the reserves—they were involved in everything.

Chico Mendes was engaged at every moment through the union. He was also the key figure in every aspect of the internal discussions here in the state. I traveled with Chico to Feijóo and to Cruzeiro do Sul to organize; then we went to Rondônia, to Ariquemes, to organize the Encontros. Chico played a major role the entire time, in everything. For example, in the increase from one to six schools in 1983, Chico wanted to help out as a teacher, but Ronaldo, Mary, and I convinced him that he was more needed as a regional leader—he was a natural leader—and if he went to live in São Pedro, the seringueiros would lose the special gift he had of bringing people together in dialogue. He was also a city councilman in Xapuri at the time. We all agreed that the most important thing for Chico was to further consolidate his leadership. He was always present at meetings; he always discussed with me and others the school project, the land issue, the reserves; he was absolutely central, and nothing was done without him.

All of this was taking place in the shadow of the dictatorship, and it impacted our work profoundly. To give you an idea, there was an empate on May 1, 1982, where there was a school, the Nova Esperança school, in the colocação Mato Grosso, seringal Santa Fé, and the ranchers wanted to destroy all the family settlements around the school. The seringueiros decided to stand up against this destruction, and they staged an empate with more than 100 men, women, children, grandparents, the whole community. Ronaldo, Raimundo de Barros, and I went there to help with the mobilization. When we arrived, the police were already beating people up, but we were the ones they were most interested in because we were union and Projeto Seringueiro leaders. We were arrested for inciting workers to revolt with Chico Mendes. Of course, we were helping the seringueiros mobilize, but not with arms; the empate movement was always nonviolent, though violence was often used against us. As the police moved to arrest the three of us, everyone present formed a human chain, declaring that the authorities were either going to take all or none, so they took us all to jail, everyone. The police had to borrow two large trucks from the ranch to transport us all to Xapuri. When we arrived, the townspeople and the church had organized a candlelight vigil, which they held all night in order to prevent violence against us. We were released shortly afterward. Certainly we were affected by the dictatorship, because the ranchers and the police worked together with the government to promote the ranchers' interests.

Getting back to the impact of the Encontro Nacional, as soon as it was over, there was a move to establish more schools, so early in 1986 CTA/Projeto Seringueiro sponsored a second training course that greatly increased the supply of teachers. Now that the extractive reserves were a real possibility, we anticipated that other communities would want to have schools. This second teacher training course drew seringueiros from other regions of Xapuri for capacity building. That was when Binho Marques, currently the governor of Acre, entered Projeto Seringueiro, but not yet as a team member. I knew Binho because we both belonged to the underground Communist Party, which I will tell you more about later. He was the party's historian, and I invited him to talk to the teachers about the history of Acre.

The teacher training course was in 1986, but in 1985 during the Encontro I met a Dutch priest, Padre João Derickx, who had lived in Nicaragua and was now living in Amazonas on the Juruá, the same river that bathes Cruzeiro do Sul here in Acre. Today he works in a parish on the outskirts of Belém do Pará. Back then he was organizing the seringueiros, and he asked for our help with an education project. I sent Pedro

Teles, who was a teacher at the Projeto Seringueiro school in Pimenteira, to do a teacher exchange there. Others came to help, too: someone named Joacyr from MEB (Movimento de Educação de Base), a church-sponsored group long dedicated to popular education, very similar to Paulo Freire. And in 1986 I wanted to consolidate the work of the National Rubber Tappers' Council throughout the Amazon states, so I went to help out in Amazonas, too.

I left CTA/Projeto Seringueiro in 1986 after I gave the teacher training course. Dercy and I moved to Carabarí where we worked with Padre João for the next four years, making the *cartilha* (text) called *Ribeirinho* (Riverbank Dweller), using the generative words that were appropriate for that location, and doing the same type of work we had done in Projeto Seringueiro. When we first arrived, Carabarí was not part of an extractive reserve, but as a result of their literacy and mobilization efforts, they were by the time we left. Dercy and I were helpful to them because we provided a model they could use, and the fact that we lived there with them and accompanied them throughout the process made a difference. Padre João later wrote a book about his experiences titled *Juruá o rio que chora* (*Juruá, the River that Cries*). Dercy and I worked there as part of the technical team of the MEB, doing teacher training and capacity building.

Between 1989 and 1992 when I was away, there was a large jump in the number of Projeto Seringueiro schools. After Chico's assassination in 1988 the extractive reserves were officially decreed, PT membership grew, and the demand for schools soared. Almost overnight the number jumped from eight to 20-odd. The adults saw education as something that would help them in the political struggle. At that time, in order to run for a position in the union it was necessary to sign your name to a document from the Ministry of Work as proof of literacy. However, since many of our most active leaders could neither read or write, they enrolled in order to learn enough to enable them to run for office. They really didn't want formal learning for themselves; that was something they wanted for their children.

At that point, 1989, Pingo Ferreira entered CTA/Projeto Seringueiro with a new team to begin working on an educational plan that would serve children in the new reserves and build upon the problem-posing education that Projeto Seringueiro was known for. I worked with him on that, too, when I returned in 1992. We wanted to have a plan in place for the anticipated schools that would prepare students to understand both their own world and that outside the forest. We wanted to give them a sound base so they could continue their education outside the seringal if they wished. They could do so if we taught them how to make social use of their learning—to be able to read, write, question, and evaluate a brief text.

We were not going to create a different model for children but rather use the elements that we already had in the adult school. However, we did read early education theorists such as Piaget; Vigotsky; an Argentine disciple of Vigotsky, Emilia Ferreiro; and others who were advocating a reflective and liberating education for children and adolescents. So we began to integrate material from that perspective into our material for literacy and postliteracy. That was the model Projeto Seringueiro had for moving from adult literacy to education for children, but the federal government, as is often the case, did not come through with the promised funds and implementation procedures for health and education in the reserves.

In the courses for teachers we would work with them in the same way that they work with their own students. Afterward, we would go to the school in the middle of the forest and spend weeks, even months visiting and supporting the teachers and their communities. In the forest, things didn't work like in a formal school, which had Portuguese first period, math second, and so on. Instead, we worked in an integrated manner; the significance of that approach is that students come to see everything as interrelated, because the subject matter of life is integrated. We also try to motivate students with texts—for example, the *Mala de Leitura* [Suitcase of Readings]—which Cila Pereira worked on; she's now with EMBRAPA, the federal government research organization. In the training courses we used the texts that the teachers themselves produced in the workshops; afterward they would work in their own classrooms to help students create and illustrate their own books also. The Projeto Seringueiro team did minimal editing; those books are good.

I continued with CTA/Projeto Seringueiro until 1999 when Binho Marques became secretary of education after Jorge Viana was elected governor. Binho invited me to work for the government on a project called Escolativa [Active School]; the idea was for the work we had done in CTA/Projeto Seringueiro between 1992 and 1996 to become public policy, but still shaped by our input. I was in favor of the idea, but Pingo was opposed because he didn't think that we could move successfully from a small-scale to a large-scale operation since so much of our success depended on the individual attention and extensive follow-up we gave our teachers.

Binho had gone to Colombia in 1996 when he was municipal secretary; there he became acquainted with the work of Escolativa and brought back various materials to study. This was at the same time that some of us in the CTA were thinking that our work might be better assumed by the state. We presented some ideas to Jorge Viana's government about how that might happen, but Pingo didn't think it was workable. I, however, wanted to work on Escolativa because it was a model that had a lot in common with Projeto Seringueiro, so in 1999 I left to work with Binho Marques.

The CTA, I'm sorry to say, seemed to be out of ideas; it had nothing more to offer. Today we have an open state for introducing innovations coming from civil society. This is very different from the hostile conditions under which we began. Many of those who were working for socially progressive NGOs before are now part of the government, leaving some NGOs, like CTA, trying to define a new role for themselves.

I went to work in rural education with Chiquinha da Silva, the director. She had written her master's thesis on Projeto Seringueiro and had worked for a year as part of the CTA/Projeto Seringueiro team. Shortly after I began there, the state initiated the very first indigenous education program, which they asked me to direct as a separate area. So, after a transition year I began working as director of indigenous education for the state in 2000.

It is interesting to see that in indigenous education I carry out projects based on my work with Projeto Seringueiro, which has been an ongoing influence. The experiences of CPI, an organization linked to the Catholic Church that works with indigenous peoples, and of Projeto Seringueiro have both been very good. Neither the Indian nor the seringueiro needs a formal school—that is, along the city model. So we began working with the Indians trying to discover their overarching tradition,

ss of education, and from that base create a pedagogy
d according to an academic year or graded levels or dis-
ntegrated and works with projects, similar to Projeto Ser-
colativa. Instead of having an academic year of the usual
200 days, the Escolativa respects the rhythm of the student who has to
work, tend the crops, and help the family. If he drops out and can only
return the next year, the work that he has done is taken into considera-
tion. Another interesting thing about the Escolativa is that their materials are more for consulting and for reference; they are not the usual
text with questions and answers. Their materials are all created by the
teacher and the student together. This is exactly what we did in Projeto
Seringueiro, when students produced their own books. That's when
school becomes a living thing.

My Projeto Seringueiro experiences have made their way into the
type of educational work that I am doing now. Indigenous education is
not a gift of the government; it is a conquest by the Indians themselves.
That conquest began with the Constitution of 1988. Until then, all official documents, the Constitution, the Lei de Diretrizes e Bases de Educação, said that the role of the school was to transform the Indian into
a non-Indian. Subsequent documents say that the role of education is to
help preserve and recover traditional cultures.

All this notwithstanding, in 1999 when Jorge Viana's government
came into office, there was nothing, just a determination on his part to
give voice to the populations that had historically been marginalized.
The indigenous population of 17,000 represents less than 1% of the
population, very little. In the years that I have been here I have proceeded
much in the same way as I did with the seringueiros. The main differ-
ences are the bilingual materials and the task of cultural rescue, which is
much larger than with the seringueiros. We are working mostly with the
Kaxinawá, who compose more than 50% of the indigenous population
of the state. We have three linguistic families; the dominant one is *pana,*
but we have produced materials even in the languages that no longer have
any social use because no one speaks them, but we have rescued them so
that they may be studied. Rescue and rehabilitation are very important
aspects of indigenous education.

When I was at CTA/Projeto Seringueiro with Pingo, we also did a project of rehabilitation for teachers. For example, lay, or uncertified, teachers

used to receive a provisional contract and a very low salary because they had no formal training, but they had the capacity to become certified. When I began working for the state, the federal government had just created a certification program for all uncertified rural teachers. Our secretariat of education was in contact with those who had created the federal program, called Pro-Formação, and they said that the teachers from Projeto Seringueiro were the most critical and disciplined because the other teachers simply had not developed a critical sense or disciplined work habits. That was important because Pro-Formação had a very large problem-solving component to it. It was also very intensive; the teachers studied all day long, and at night they had a lot of homework. Those who did not have the habit of studying, who were not disciplined, did not do their homework for the next day. On the weekend they would play soccer, but the Projeto Seringueiro teachers, since it was an intensive formation course, studied day and night, and they completed the rigorous course in the allotted 45 days, performing better than all the other candidates.

In 2007 the government sponsored a program to train rural teachers at the university level as well. They all participated in that first certification phase of roughly fourth to eighth grade, and of that group, about five or six stopped there, leaving 40 who took the college entrance exam, and we have 30 or 32 who are studying at the university, mostly at the branch in Xapuri. They are studying math, history, geography, biology, and pedagogy, for example. Thus, those who were lay, or uncertified, teachers—many of whom first were students of Projeto Seringueiro themselves in a place in the seringal where there had never before been a school—are now studying at the university.

Today many more seringueiros are staying in the seringal; they have a much more critical worldview, and they perceive how important their work is because deforestation continues to devastate new areas every day. I think those who have chosen to remain offer a great example, because previous governments dismantled the way of life of the seringueiro; they disabled him. There is no more rubber, rubber has no more value, so the challenge for him becomes to learn from the forest again. There are many prominent examples: Júlio Barbosa, who became mayor of Xapuri; Raimundo de Barros, of Projeto Seringueiro and the union who remained, became city councilman and state senator; also João Sena, Zé Conde, Ti Doca. These are very active, politically and environmentally aware people

who have chosen to live in the seringal because they know it is important that the forest remain standing; they defend it by staying.

There are several reasons that emigration from the forest has diminished. The work of CTA/Projeto Seringueiro is one factor, but there
are many. It's easy to think, *Ah, people are leaving because there is no school
there,* but that's not correct. At times people leave a place where there is
a school, and do not leave a place where there is no school. They leave
because of isolation, because there is no way to market their product,
and because of health factors. The main thing is that a community has
a project for itself. For example, in some communities in the extractive
reserves, students are learning seed management. It is important schoolwork, and certainly one who is involved in that project does not migrate
out of his community. But if you have an isolated area that does not have
these conditions, people leave, either to go to the city or to another community that offers better living conditions.

The question of gender has from the beginning been important for
CTA/Projeto Seringueiro. The world of the seringueiro is very, very
machista because of the way in which the occupation of Acre took place.
Those who came were single, and women were just objects in the beginning, merchandise. The seringueiro who produced a lot of rubber
could buy a woman. But from the beginning of Projeto Seringueiro we
had leaders like Dercy, Marlete, Mary, and women who were teacher
trainers. Don't forget that Dercy was president of the syndicate for a
while, and that she was a teacher. She began the tradition of having
everyone attend a common syndicate meeting. Before, the men would
come to talk and the women would go to the kitchen. Dercy would not
permit this, saying, "We are all going to the meeting!" Also, in Projeto
Seringueiro schools, when the coordinating team would hold teacher-
training courses, we never had a gendered division of labor. It is true that
there are cases of resistance, but today people perceive clearly that when
there is a meeting of any kind in the seringal there will be many women
participating. Another thing is the large number of extremely active
women as union members, teachers, and cooperative members. Before,
these activities were restricted to men. The model is very machista,
change is slow, but I think that CTA/Projeto Seringueiro has played an
important part. We have all worked for this, that men and women think
of themselves as equal.

Many influences and experiences have shaped my work he
The first was liberation theology and the option for the poor, a
by Dom Moacyr. But I would say that the intellectual inspiration for
the other priests and visiting faculty here in Rio Branco while I was a
novitiate was Marxism. Padre Cláudio Deustro had a strong influence on
me. He studied with Dom Moacyr and they are close friends, but they
are very different. Padre Cláudio brought faculty from the university in
Rio Branco (UFAC) who were very committed Marxists, including the
Italian padre Paulo Abaloni. We also read Marx, Gramsci, Lenin, and
studied the history of the Russian Revolution. When I left the seminary,
what stayed with me was the social doctrine of the church, the papal
bulls, and, above all, the decisions of the bishops in Medellín. They were
like a Bible for us; we carried them around in our backpacks. Yes, above
all, the Medellín documents. I still have them.

When I left the seminary, there were two important political influences beginning to take shape: the Workers Party (PT) and the Communist Party of Brazil (PCdoB); the latter had a messianic orientation
because its members saw Marxist revolution as a salvation. You have to
remember the extreme political context in order to understand this.
PCdoB at one time was Maoist, but in my time they had abandoned
Maoism for the Albanian model. I rejected the Albanian tendency, saying that Marxism in Brazil should be read and applied differently, adapted
to our own situation. What we wanted in the PRC (Partido Revolu-
cionario Comunista) was a democratic reopening within PCdoB. Other
PRC members besides myself at that time were Binho Marques, Marina
Silva, Raimundo de Barros, Chico Mendes, Gumercindo Clóvis, and Júlio
Barbosa to a lesser extent. Nearly everyone who was in PT or in the stu-
dent movement in Rio Branco at that time belonged to the Communist
Party. Participation was clandestine because the party was outlawed.
Most of the PCdoB members who thought like I did passed on to the
New Left.

Even today I think that Marx has intellectual contributions for us:
his reading of class divisions, his idea of the dialectic, that people can
generate a positive force through antagonism. And, of course, we can
learn a lot from the mistakes of Marxism. Most of the errors were not
made by Marx, but his followers. When you see terrible deviations from
Marxism, like Stalinism, you learn from those mistakes. Lenin was a

good strategist, very intelligent, he knew how to apply strategy during the Russian Revolution. But the theories of Marx and Lenin studied separately and out of context are not helpful. What is helpful is to read Walter Benjamin to help understand and criticize Marxism; also Rosa Luxembourg, Lukacs, and Gramsci. The national PT in Brazil took intellectual and ideological inspiration from these figures, but they made some very unfortunate detours in applying them. I continue with these convictions, studying Marxism, and exchanging ideas with Eloisa Winter of UFAC, and Reginaldo Castelo, who worked briefly with the CTA and is now working with the Landless Movement, *Sem Terra,* outside of Acre. These two have exposed me to many readings on Marxism in India, Asia, the United States, and England.

I had already read Paulo Freire in Fortaleza, Ceará, before coming here because as a seminarian I had participated in the workers pastorate. We had a French priest who was our spiritual director at the seminary in Ceará, and he was active in the workers' pastorate. He was a *padre secular,* not in any order, and he introduced me to Freire's *Pedagogy of the Oppressed* in 1976, when Freire was in exile. Freire was the intellectual inspiration that brought me to Projeto Seringueiro, because the first text *Poronga* was very Freireian in inspiration.

As you know, CEDI, the Freireian educational NGO in São Paulo, advised us closely in the creation of *Poronga.* They came here, worked with us, and did a study to determine the generative words. It was extremely difficult to work here in the conditions we faced, so it was very important to have the support of CEDI and Freire himself, with whom we worked to systematize the text. I even wrote a poem honoring Freire on his visit to Rio Branco and Xapuri in 1983. CEDI was like a consultant for us; whenever things weren't going well we corresponded with them. At one time, Ronaldo Lima de Oliveira, one of the teachers and founders of the CTA, was at a roundtable with them on adult education. Sérgio Haddad, who was with CEDI and today is with the NGO Ação Educativa [Educational Action], was there. Also with CEDI then and now with Ação Educativa are Rando Joia and Vera Masagão. They were here with me in Acre helping until 1984; they corresponded, phoned, gave advice, and went back and forth consulting. DiGorgio would come to help us, I don't remember his first name; at that time he was a student;

today he is a professor at UNICAMP in São Paulo. Regina Hara came to Acre and lived here for three years, staying in the seringal. She has since passed away, but her influence was very important. Freire and CEDI were central influences. None of us in the original group were educators. We learned as we went, and we were fortunate to have CEDI to help us.

Ronaldo Lima de Oliveira has been a continuing influence for me. Before teaching in Projeto Seringueiro, he had been an indigenist with FUNAI, the government Indian protection agency, but during the 1970s FUNAI became militarized and there was a great persecution and purge of indigenists. Ronaldo resigned from FUNAI in protest against the firing of other indigenists and went to live in the seringal. When he left FUNAI he was accused of organizing guerrilla activities among the Apuriñā Indians in Boca do Acre. He was, in fact, a great admirer of Che Guevara, and he loved reading his *Diaries;* he also read Lenin.

For the past 12 years, Ronaldo has had this place in Xapuri where he is working in ecologically degraded areas, enriching them without burning, proving that four hectares can yield a good quality of life for a family, economic and food security, produce fruits and all types of foods for consumption and for market. He is showing that you can make a living and reforest destroyed areas. The forestry engineer said that it was not possible, for example, to plant mahogany except in forest conditions, that you couldn't transport and transplant seedlings that had fallen to the forest floor. Ronaldo, however, has done just that and now has a sapling bank. He has taken seedlings that don't have enough sun to thrive in the dense forest, and transplanted them to a controlled area that favors their growth. His demonstration area is about two hours from here by car. He, Armando Soares Filho, and I want to transform this demonstration area into a school for seringueiro children who have completed the fourth grade but can't continue at present because there are no schools; they could learn this new way of managing wood in their colocações and learn not to deforest or burn.

I was shocked, horrified—it had been a long time since I had been to the seringal—when I went to visit Ronaldo and saw many, many rubber tree areas that I had known before now turned into small cattle ranches! With the seringueiros going hungry, they are cutting down the forest and converting it to pasture, but cattle raising does not give returns. If we are able to implant the idea of the Escolativa, adolescents will have the knowledge and the conviction to plant and help their family colocação. Ronaldo is very creative and always responding to the needs he sees around him. Armando is also an indigenist who resigned in protest against the firings at FUNAI. Later there was an amnesty and they both returned, but Ronaldo is older and soon retired, while Armando still has a few more years to go, then he will dedicate himself to this project, too.

By the way, Projeto Seringueiro also influenced the work of the indigenists. For example, CPI—which is the NGO that works with the Indians—the first text they used for the education of indigenous teachers was *Poronga* without any adaptation whatsoever, the same generative terms, the same discussion, because at that time, the Indian was a seringueiro.

Chico Mendes was a tremendous example for me. The church—in particular, liberation theology—was a major influence for Chico as it was for most of us. I first met Chico when he would pass through Rio Branco and stay at the seminary and have lunch with us. He was very, very close to the padres in Xapuri. He was not a pastoral agent or a churchgoer, but he stayed with us, and I admired the way he encouraged people to organize in base communities. These all became associated with the union, then with the Workers Party (PT). There was a complete symbiosis between the two; just to give you an idea, we would begin and end a Workers Party meeting with the Lord's Prayer. That's no longer the case, for liberation theology is no longer a point of reference in the Acrean church; now there is the charismatic moment, much more individualistic, introspective, not social. My own influences now are not so much Christianity, but indigenism. I am studying the works of anthropologists who are indigenists.

Ideas and influences change over time. For example, after the opposition—that is, all the organizations of civil society, teachers, students, domestic workers, and many others involved in the social movement, including the PT—gained power in the 1990s, some people lost their way. We won within a capitalist system and during a time of globalization and neoliberalism, which we have to keep in mind, but I do not agree with those who want to turn all work with the Indians over to

NGOs because, to the degree that you transfer state functions to an NGO, you minimize what should be state responsibilities. I work for the government now, but I came up through the NGOs, and they have a different role—to pressure, to be a critical voice. Indigenous education today is a state function only because my team has been working since 1999 to bring people, many of them colleagues, around to a public way of thinking that this is the responsibility of the state. Conservative pressure groups have too much influence; they want to move too many things to NGOs, and some people in government have lost their bearings. For example, in the areas of environment and education there are huge NGOs whose functions should be transferred to the state. On the eve of the first administration of Jorge Viana, I produced a document for UNICEF—which had financed various NGOs, including the CTA—saying that the role of the CTA is supplemental because the state is not doing it, but when the state is able, it should.

In some cases the state assumed responsibilities, but in others they decided not to develop competencies because they could buy those services. For example, in the case of Projeto Seringueiro, we created a competency in the area of extractive education that was special, but neither we in the CTA nor the government knew how to dialogue with each other, so it didn't move forward, and the government ended up instead buying expensive services for education from grades five through eight, from the Fundação Roberto Marino, an NGO connected to TV Globo. It's crazy because we can develop local competencies right here. There are things like this that make me think there is a disconnect in the government's thinking.

The government apparatus itself makes people change their ideas, their ethics, but we did not win a government through revolution but through democratic election, and this is the structure that we have to work within. However, the government should attend to all classes, and not just the wealthiest, that is the problem. There are some people I have worked with for years who are committed to the poor and who haven't changed, like Binho Marques; his commitment hasn't wavered. But the power of persuasion of a big producer who wants to build a highway or export cattle is much greater than that of a rural community that needs to build a small, dirt access road. We have the power to administer the state, not redo it, so inevitably we face limitations. I have friends who were one with us in the past, but who now have changed their thinking and want to exploit lumber and oil, and build dams for hydroelectric power. Social and environmental considerations, including the dislocation of indigenous peoples, are no longer primary concerns to them. I also think the Alcobras program of devoting more land to the production of sugar cane for use as fuel is a disaster because rural workers are being forced to choose between producing sugar cane or relocating. There are people who were very involved in the social movement of the 1980s with me who think this is good thing, a natural evolution. I would say at the very least 15% of the people with whom I converse and work have changed their mind along these lines.

Meanwhile, I try to keep my ethical sense and my ideals intact and in practice. I made a personal commitment to begin working with indigenous communities in 1999; before that, absolutely nothing had been done. But we have placed 74 indigenous teachers who are now providing instruction in the interior, and we have trained them through the *ensino médio,* not just *ensino básico.* This year we are actually going to have a special university course designed for the preparation of indigenous teachers. We have now prepared 52 more, in addition to the 74. That's because of the intervention of the state. We had support from Binho when he was secretary of education so we could develop these competencies and attend to these communities. It would be terrible to transfer this to NGOs, especially since we have accomplished so much, not to mention all the good that has been done in the general area of rural education through the government.

My biggest challenges now are to help indigenous teachers gain admission to the university, and to keep on forming indigenous teachers. Another is to have a category recognizing indigenous teachers and to have the Escolativa recognized. The indigenous school is neither rural nor urban, it needs its own category; so do indigenous teachers—they're different, they're bilingual mostly, they teach a little differently, and they can't be treated just like other teachers.

I should point out another very important and early intellectual influence that has left a lasting imprint. I came here to Acre already having had a very profound liberation theology experience in Ceará, the "theology of the hoe," it was called. The best-known advocate is the Belgian-born priest, José Comblin. Also the German priest there in Ceará, Alfred Kuntz, who was a tremendous example to me. "Alfredinho" took a vow of complete poverty and actually chose to make his living with the hoe. There was a very progressive bishop in Ceará, Antônio Fragoso, who participated in the movement *Justiça e Paz* [Justice and Peace], which had as one of its objectives the freeing of political prisoners. Dom Fragoso was very open, and he accepted the idea of having a seminarian, myself, study ecology and have the practical experience of the theology of the hoe. Of course I was deeply impressed by the work of Archbishop Dom Helder Câmara throughout the Northeast. I also was influenced by the Peruvian Gustavo Gutiérrez's *Liberation Theology;* I was moved by the tragic story of the Colombian priest Camilo Torres; I read the French theologian Teilhard de Chardin. It was a time of great intellectual ferment and solidarity with the poor, and Ceará was a center of liberation theology. After I came to Acre, certainly Leonardo and Clodovis Boff were very influential figures for me; they gave external courses at the seminary, and Clodovis lived there with us for a while. On reflection, I see how these factors have converged to influence who I am and what I believe. They have, in turn, found expression in my work with Projeto Seringueiro and indigenous education. ✣

Part III
Conclusion

Conclusion

Introduction

What can we say now about Projeto Seringueiro, and what lessons can educators, environmentalists, religious and social reformers, and NGOs learn from it? First, despite the fact that Projeto Seringueiro faced huge obstacles from the outset—a hostile and often violent political environment, poor funding, no trained teachers, a culture among the rubber tappers that totally lacked schooling and literacy, and an economic and social situation in which the seringueiros were accustomed to harsh oppression and debt peonage—it succeeded amazingly well. It was an extremely effective popular education movement whose basic principles and goals have become mainstream public policy. The project's influence continues to expand like ripples in a pond. As Antonia Pereira, a longtime teacher from Xapuri, comments, "The knowledge that comes from Projeto Seringueiro has extended outward. The ideas, ethics, and methodology behind Projeto Seringueiro are now everywhere, in former students and teachers."

Second, education based on the culture and habitat of the community can be empowering. Projeto Seringueiro changed the lives of many rubber tappers by giving them opportunities to develop powers they did not know they had. It also helped them value their own knowledge of the forest and their way of life, and from that basis of confidence to analyze and criticize the views of the political and economic elite long thought to be irresistible. In short, Projeto Seringueiro helped enable the rubber tappers to become effective members of civil society. This is an important point, because the usual assumption is that those with limited formal education are neither intelligent nor articulate, much less eloquent in presenting an argument or defending their rights.

History of Projeto Seringueiro

The story of Projeto Seringueiro from founding to institutionalization is complex and often inspiring. Its history falls roughly into three stages. The first began in 1981 as an emergency effort to impart rudimentary literacy and numeracy skills to exploited seringueiros in their struggle for economic survival. This stage lasted until 1986, by which time the project was in disarray. In the first stage, the main problems Project Rubber Tapper faced were a dangerous, lawless political environment, and a lack of schools, teachers, staff, and materials.

The second phase was one of refounding began under Binho Marques, who, at Chico Mendes's behest, revived the project and expanded the number of schools. The greatest difficulty of this period was the lack of prepared teachers to keep up with the jump in the number of schools, and the devastating blow of Mendes's assassination in December 1988. The loss of their dynamic leader completely sapped the morale of those involved in Projeto Seringueiro.

Mendes's death dealt a staggering but not a mortal blow to the movement. This is a useful observation for those in development studies and those working in the field. Projeto Seringueiro was an organic, authentic, popular, broadly based grassroots organization, itself part of a widespread mobilization effort throughout the Amazon during the 1970s and 1980s. It was not an imposition from the outside, nor was it a top-down affair. The entire rural population was mobilized during the period because of the effective work of the base communities, the union, and, in the Projeto Seringueiro schools, because of Freire's participatory, egalitarian pedagogy and the dedication of unusually talented individuals. Thus, when Chico Mendes was assassinated, Projeto Seringueiro, and the larger movement of which it was a significant component, did not die with him. After a time of grief, shock, and disarray, others picked up the fallen standard and carried forward the work of the schools and the movement.

The third and final phase was roughly between 1992 and 2008, when an official ceremony took place honoring Projeto Seringueiro and transferring its remaining eight schools to the state. This often troubled period was one of gradual absorption by the state of Acre both of personnel and materials developed by Projeto Seringueiro. The absorption process became a virtual brain drain from 1999 when Jorge Viana, himself once director of the CTA, Projeto Seringueiro's umbrella organization, became governor.

Throughout its history, one observes the intersection of several powerful intellectual influences that informed, to varying degrees, both Projeto Seringueiro and the larger social movement of which it was an important part: the pedagogy of Paulo Freire, liberation theology, aspects of Marxism, and of course, environmentalism, which underlay every aspect of the project and has been its most visible contribution. We have observed the interwoven strands of these influences in every voice that has spoken to us, perhaps nowhere more clearly integrated than in the life and work of Manoel Estébio Cavalcante da Cunha, who himself recognized the confluence of all these factors in his decisions to work first as a seminarian, then as organizer, educator, environmentalist, political activist with Marxist leanings, and voice both of rubber tappers and indigenous populations of the entire Amazon region.

Freire's intellectual presence is seen at every point, including at the beginning, when he personally advised Projeto Seringueiro's founders. An emphasis on local culture; the value of local knowledge; interactive teaching; open, problem-posing questions to promote critical reflection and praxis; education for political participation—these were the defining features of Freire's pedagogy as practiced in Projeto Seringueiro. One can see this influence especially in Pingo Ferreira's absorbing account of the preparation and invaluable accompaniment of Projeto Seringueiro teachers as well as Manoel da Cunha's recounting of intellectual influences in his own life. Freire's presence is like an invisible hand guiding alternative education not only in Acre but throughout Brazil and beyond. His pedagogy influenced community leaders, including those in base communities, often without their realizing it; likewise, educational and social reformers had internalized Freire's basic points by the 1980s.

Liberation theology was influential in Projeto Seringueiro because it provided a much needed message of hope for the literally dispossessed through its emphasis on the social gospel and discussion of Bible passages that speak of God's compassion for the marginalized of society. The Catholic Church in Acre, exemplifying the "preferential option for the poor," helped the rubber tappers' union (STR) coordinate the dangerous empates between unarmed seringueiros and powerful ranchers, their hired gunmen, and the police who did the ranchers' bidding. As Manoel da Cunha points out, many Projeto Seringueiro teachers and students were among the union members and church monitors who were arrested and beaten in such confrontations. The church offered sanctuary to persecuted rubber tappers and defended their claims to the land through the Pastoral Land Commission (CPT) and Bishop Dom Moacyr Grechi's intervention. Further, church-sponsored leadership training workshops imparted valuable consciousness-raising, communication, and organizational skills to leaders of the social movement like Ivanilde Lopes da Silva, as well as to teachers in Projeto Seringueiro, such as Dercy Teles and Antonia Pereira.

Marxism contributed its class analysis and emphasis on the need for workers to organize, a lesson that Chico Mendes learned early. The influence of Marxism is seen in the work of many university faculty and journalists in Acre, in the kind of liberation theology embraced by many priests in Xapuri, in the development of Binho Marques and Manoel da Cunha, and in the language and vocabulary of the syndicate movement and the Workers' Party (PT). The Marxist influence was of the flexible variety. The less rigid the ideology, the more acceptance it found among seringueiros. As Binho Marques points out, when one dogmatic Marxist came to Acre preaching revolution, he was quickly seen as absurd. A goal of the union was to create a sense of class solidarity among individualistic seringueiros, though it was always an uphill battle since they persisted in regarding themselves as seringueiros rather than workers, thus defining themselves more by occupation than by class. At least as important as Marxism itself was the iconic figure of Che Guevara, who inspired Marxists and non-Marxists alike throughout Latin America and elsewhere at the time.

Thus, Projeto Seringueiro's history incarnates by way of practical application through lived experience the intertwined progressive intellectual strands of the period, employing them to assist seringueiros in empowering themselves and defending the forest.

Reasons for Success

The project has faced such intractable obstacles that one wonders how it succeeded at all. There are many reasons, but chief among them are the dedicated, realistic idealists who recognized the urgency of the situation in 1981, and who mobilized seringueiros and nonseringueiros alike into extremely effective partnerships based on respect and mutuality. Here Chico Mendes's extraordinary openness to cooperation with like-minded allies was essential. From the beginning, Mendes and the seringueiros knew what they wanted, and collaborators understood what that was: empowerment at the most basic level of economic survival. Mendes's clarity of objective and his desire to reach out to advisory groups are apparent in the reason he gave for the success of the first school in Nazaré: "The most important aspect of this school that helped us strengthen our cause is that we did not accept a school with the political orientation of the official [educational] system. We looked for people that really had a base in popular education that was different from what one usually sees in this country."[1]

Projeto Seringueiro thus succeeded in part because, in the beginning, leaders like Mendes sought the assistance of NGOs like CEDI, which was Freireian in orientation and had experience in popular education and base communities; the NGOs, in turn, embraced the goals of the seringueiros.

Another reason for Projeto Seringueiro's success is its emphasis on developing critical problem-solving skills through open discussion of community themes. This is the basic Freireian principle, and it illustrates the root values of equality and collegiality/community inherent in the method: No one learns alone. Constant discussion of common issues, such as how to make the cooperative work, thus served to produce articulate, reflective individuals who became accustomed to constructing arguments, and to listening and responding to the arguments of others in a dialogue among equals, even as they learned to read and write. This was the exact opposite of the silence, intimidation, resignation, and hopeless isolation that had prevailed among the rubber tappers in the past. The seringueiros' skills in communication and argumentation were put to use in 1985 at the first Rubber Tappers Encounter in Brasília, where the tappers themselves, many of them Projeto Seringueiro teachers and students who had never before left their own seringal, successfully put the argument for extractive reserves before the assembled public officials.

In addition, Projeto Seringueiro succeeded because the teachers learned in their training workshops that disciplined study and critical analysis pay off. It is difficult to overestimate the value of these training sessions. For example, Projeto Seringueiro teachers turned out to be far and away the superior students in the problem-solving-based certification courses for lay rural teachers given by the state in 2000.

The project has also been successful because teachers and coordinators have consistently foregrounded the environmental component of its curriculum; if anything, it has become even more pronounced over time, as teacher Antonia Pereira points out in her interview. In fact, this may become the most important legacy of Projeto Seringueiro: its contribution to an informed defense of the rainforest environment by involved citizens. The Projeto Seringueiro experience has prepared residents of Xapuri to confront their most recent environmental challenge, cited by union president and former Projeto Seringueiro teacher Dercy Teles: the blatant deforestation and loss of habitat caused by the sugar-cane biofuel industry that is proliferating throughout the Amazon.

Overall then, the project has succeeded because it has imparted practical and analytical skills, been a force for community mobilization and defense of the forest, and significantly improved the quality of life for seringueiros.[2]

Projeto Seringueiro is a microcosm of the wider struggle that began in the Amazon in the mid-1960s, continued through the decades of destruction in the 1970s and 1980s, and still exists today, though in a different form. Projeto Seringueiro succeeded because, as a consequence of this broader struggle, there has occurred a political turning of tables in Acre and Brazil as a whole. One result is that the philosophy and accomplishments of Projeto Seringueiro have attained official status in Acre. However, with that institutionalization has come the realization that bureaucratization is eroding the special partnerships of mutuality that have been so successful and have characterized the NGO in the past, replacing them in some instances with special interests and the desire to benefit personally as Chiquinha da Silva observed in her interview.

Lessons of Projeto Seringueiro and Larger Truths

Several important lessons emerge from the Projeto Seringueiro experience. First, education should be empowering, whether one lives in the Amazon rainforest or the inner city of Chicago. Empowerment, however, is something that educational bureaucracies are often unable or unwilling to promote. Without it, educational reform is likely to fail. Second, genuine partnerships between educational experts and the community are critical. Professionals can provide the expertise, but the community has to supply the fundamental goals; each needs to respect and support the other. Third, the curriculum has to be relevant to the expressed needs of the population served, which should be intimately involved in shaping it. Fourth, teachers should be drawn from the local population insofar as possible; where such an organic connection is not possible, teachers should be well acquainted with the history, social dynamics, and culture of the community. Fifth, both the personnel and the curriculum must be flexible, adjusting quickly to changing conditions. Sixth, education must promote community, not only in its curriculum but also in its activities and in the way that teachers and administrators relate to each other and to ordinary people. Seventh, the practice of accompaniment is crucial; teachers need to be supported onsite through frequent and extended visitation by sympathetic and experienced staff.

Projected onto a larger canvas, we can see that the educational lessons learned from Projeto Seringueiro reveal deeper human truths that are at once reassuring and troubling. First, the reassuring truths: Projeto Seringueiro provides a textbook example of meaningful, democratic social change carried out by small groups working together. It is hard to imagine that Projeto Seringueiro would have taken off, much less expanded, without the galvanizing leadership of Chico Mendes and a few key colleagues who worked very closely with him. Mendes was a seringueiro himself. He spoke and dressed like a seringueiro, and he shared the same background as all other seringueiros. He was from Xapuri, he was poor, and he was one of them. But he was much more than that, too, because he had a particular genius for reaching out and forming partnerships with other groups—local, national, and international. Mendes, like his key colleagues Raimundo de Barros, Mary Allegretti, Manoel da Cunha, Binho Marques, among others, constantly sought alliances with technical, ecumenical, environmental, and educational NGOs in Acre and beyond. In this way, Mendes introduced seringueiros to the outside world and the outside world to the seringueiros.

The second reassuring truth of Projeto Seringueiro is that it brought about internal changes in the seringueiros themselves. Because of the kind of education Projeto Seringueiro imparts, it has produced change from the inside out—that is, in affect, beliefs, and behaviors. Longtime teacher Ademir Pereira remarks, "It has changed the way of thinking of the seringueiros. . . . We don't just teach reading and writing in our schools. We also teach people how to respect each other." Nearly every voice from Projeto Seringueiro has told of observable changes in the seringueiros' self-concept and in their interactions with others. Pingo Ferreira has commented on the increased capacity of the seringueiros to relate the particular to the universal—that is, to have a fuller grasp of the world and their place in it, essential for effective participation as informed citizens, which is a fundamental objective of Freire's democratizing model. Ademir Pereira, Pingo Ferreira, Antonia Pereira, and Chiquinha da Silva all have commented that the seringueiros' enhanced self-perception and capabilities have enabled them to feel proud rather than ashamed of their oral forest culture and, in many cases, to place a greater value on preserving the forest that sustains it. Thus, Projeto Seringueiro has not only helped bring about a radical paradigm shift in the seringueiros' worldview, it has also shown that an empowering education contributes to a positive self-concept and improves the quality of social interactions.

Now for the sobering truth. The kind of independent thinking promoted by Projeto Seringueiro undermines, or at least questions, the established authority of all bureaucracies, educational and otherwise, which, not surprisingly, are rarely interested in promoting critical reflection. This situation has made the move from civil to government sector especially difficult for Projeto Seringueiro. For one thing, entrenched interests act as a heavy counterweight to impede the turning of the tables and to reverse hard-fought gains. Chiquinha da Silva and Manoel da Cunha note with frustration the brick wall of opposition they face from vested interests in the state government. Chiquinha da Silva in particular recounts the difficulty in working with those who care nothing for education or the poor, but who desire only power. Conflicts with intractable opponents form part of the daily reality now that those with a Projeto Seringueiro philosophy have moved from the smaller pond into a vortex of vested interests, and sometimes venal and incompetent actors. In this sense, Projeto Seringueiro can be seen as a cautionary tale of the price of success, or of the roiling currents that threaten to swamp the boat, as Chiquinha da Silva puts it, when an alternative project is integrated into the bureaucratic establishment.

Projeto Seringueiro survived not only the burning of the forest, intimidation, eviction, and murder of seringueiros but also a paralyzing lack of funds, trained teachers, and staff. One hopes that Projeto Seringueiro's former leaders and staff can withstand the grinding bureaucratization and top-down impositions that are the very antithesis of Projeto Seringueiro's model of education.

One is reminded of turn-of-the-twentieth-century Brazilian journalist Euclides da Cunha's apt dictum about human existence expressed in his monumental *Os Sertões* (Rebellion in the Backlands): "To live is to adapt oneself." So far, Projeto Seringueiro's former team members have shown remarkable adaptability in negotiating their new government identity, however frustrating that process may be for longtime NGO workers. Manoel da Cunha has proved adaptable indeed, and remarks in his interview that there are distinct advantages to rural and indigenous education in moving from an impoverished NGO to a government-funded program. Pingo Ferreira has said of Projeto Seringueiro, "Above all, Projeto Seringueiro has been flexible, always adapting to the realities and culture of the seringueiro." One hopes that Projeto Seringueiro's legacy of flexibility will enable its former personnel and graduates to continue turning the tables for popular empowerment through education in Acre. That would be a liberating example indeed, not just for educators or the people of Acre, but for all of us. 🌿

Notes
1. Constance Elaine Campbell, "The Role of a Popular Education Project in Mobilizing a Rural Community: A Case Study of the Rubber Tappers of Acre, Brazil" (MA thesis, University of Florida, 1990), 34–35.
2. Ibid., x–xi.

Bibliography

Interviews

Carvalho, Dercy Teles de. Interviews by author. August 1, 2007; October 8, 2008. Xapuri.

Cunha, Manoel Estébio Cavalcante da. Interviews by author. May 22, 2006; August 5, 2007; October 10, 2008. Rio Branco.

Evangelista, Raimunda. Interview by author. October 8, 2008. Xapuri.

Feitosa, Júlia. Interview by author. May 19, 2006. Rio Branco.

Ferreira, Djalcir "Pingo." Interviews by author. May 25 and 26, 2006; August 8, 9, and 10, 2007; October 5 and 6, 2008. Rio Branco.

Grechi, Moacyr. Interview by author. August 10, 2007. Rio Branco.

Lima, Salustiano Diogo de. Interview by author. October 8, 2008. Xapuri.

Marques, Arnóbio "Binho," Júnior. Interviews by author. May 22, 2006; October 8, 2008. Rio Branco.

Pereira Rodrigues, Ademir. Interview by author. May 25 and 26, 2006. Xapuri.

Pereira Vieira, Antonia. Interview by author. August 7, 2007. Xapuri.

Santos, Cila Pereira dos. Interview by author. May 18, 2006. Rio Branco.

Silva, Francisca "Chiquinha" das Chagas Souza da. Interviews by author. August 3, 2007; October 8, 2008. Rio Branco.

Silva, Ivanilde Lopes da. Interviews by author. August 8, 9, and 10, 2007; October 8 and 9, 2008. Rio Branco.

Zaire, Graciete. Interview by author. October 14, 2008. Rio Branco.

Other Sources

Adriance, Madeleine Cousineau. *Promised Land: Base Christian Communities and the Struggle for the Amazon.* Albany: State University of New York Press, 1995.

Allegretti, Mary Helena. "A Construção Social de Políticas Ambientais: Chico Mendes e o Movimento dos Seringueiros." PhD Thesis, Universidade de

159

Brasília-DF, 2002. Available online at Marina Silva Biblioteca da Floresta, http://www.ac.gov.br/bibliotecadafloresta.

———. "Reservas Extrativistas: Parâmetros para uma Política de Desenvolvimento Sustentável na Amazônia." In Arnt, ed., *O Destino da Floresta,* 17–47.

———, and Stephan Schwartzman. *Extractive Production in the Amazon and the Rubber Tappers' Movement.* Washington, DC: Environmental Defense Fund, 1987.

Almeida, Mauro William Barbosa de. "Rubber Tappers of the Upper Juruá River, Brazil." Diss., University of Cambridge, England, 1992.

———, and Mário Assis Meneses. "Acre—Reserva Extrativista do Alto Juruá." In Arnt, ed., *O Destino da Floresta,* 164–225.

Anonymous. *Guardian Weekly.* April 18, 2008.

Arnt, Ricardo, ed. *O Destino da Floresta, Reservas Extrativistas e Desenvolvimento Sustentável na Amazônia.* Rio de Janeiro: Dumará Distribuidora da Publicações Ltds. Copublished by Instituto de Estudos Amazônicos e Ambientais, Fundação Konrad Adenauer, 1994.

Aufderheide, Pat, and Bruce Rich. "Environmental Reform and the Multilateral Banks." *World Policy Journal* 5 (Spring 1988): 301–22.

Boff, Clodovis. *Deus e o Homem no Inferno Verde: Quatro Meses de Convivência com as CEBs do Acre.* Petrópolis: Vozes, 1980.

———. *Teologia Pé no Chão.* 2nd ed. Petrópolis: Vozes, 1984.

Boff, Leonardo. *Jesus Christ Liberator: A Critical Christology for Our Times.* New York: Orbis, 1978.

———, and Clodovis Boff. *Introducing Liberation Theology.* New York: Orbis, 1987.

Burdick, John. *Looking for God in Brazil.* Berkeley: University of California Press, 1993.

Campbell, Constance Elaine. "The Role of a Popular Education Project in Mobilizing a Rural Community: A Case Study of the Rubber Tappers of Acre, Brazil." MA thesis, University of Florida, 1990.

———, and the Women's Group of Xapuri. "Out on the Front Lines but Still Struggling for Voice: Women in the Rubber Tappers' Defense of the Forest in Xapuri, Acre, Brazil." In *Feminist Political Ecology: Global Issues and Local Experiences,* edited by Dianne Rocheleau, Barbara Thomas-Slayter, and Esther Wangari, 27–61. London: Routledge Press, 1996.

CTA/Projeto Seringueiro. *Proposta Político Pedagógica: um Projeto com Características Únicas para as Escolas da Floresta,* 2000, Photocopy.

Daly, Herman, and John B. Cobb Jr. *For the Common Good: Redirecting the Economy toward Community, the Environment, and a Sustainable Future.* 2nd ed. Boston: Beacon Press, 1994.

Dean, Warren. *Brazil and the Struggle for Rubber: A Study in Environmental History.* Cambridge: Cambridge University Press, 1987.

Eade, Deborah, ed. *Development and Culture.* London: Oxfam, 2002.

————. *Development Methods and Approaches: Critical Reflections.* London: Oxfam, 2003.

Edwards, Michael. *Civil Society.* London: Polity Press, 2004.

————. *Future Positive.* London: Earthscan Publications, 1999.

Escobar, Arturo. *Encountering Development: The Making and Unmaking of the Third World.* Princeton, NJ: Princeton University Press, 1995.

Farmer, Paul. *Pathologies of Power.* Berkeley: University of California Press, 2003.

Fearnside, Philip M. *Extractive Reserves in Brazilian Amazonia: An Opportunity to Maintain Tropical Rain Forest Under Sustainable Use.* Manaus: National Institute of Amazon Research, 1988.

Fisher, Julie. *Nongovernments: NGOs and the Political Development of the Third World.* West Hartford, CT: Kumarian Press, 1998.

Freire, Paulo. *Education for Critical Consciousness.* New York: Seabury Press, 1973.

————. *Education, the Practice of Freedom.* London: Writers and Readers Publishing Cooperative, 1976.

————. *Pedagogy of the Oppressed.* New York: Herder and Herder, 1970.

————, and Donaldo P. Macedo. *Literacy: Reading the Word and the World.* Critical Studies in Education Series. South Hadley, MA: Bergin & Garvey Publishers, 1987.

Gonçalves, Maria Ronizia Pereira. "A Fala Sagrada e Social do 'Todos Somos Irmãos' de 1976 a 1982." BA thesis, UFAC, 1997.

Gutiérrez, Gustavo. *A Theology of Liberation.* Maryknoll, NY: Orbis, 2003.

Hemming, John. *Tree of Rivers: The Story of the Amazon.* London: Thames and Hudson, 2008.

Hennelly, Alfred T., S.J. *Liberation Theology: A Documentary History.* New York: Orbis, 1990.

Heyck, Denis L. *Surviving Globalization in Three Latin American Communities.* Toronto: Broadview Press, 2002.

IDBAmérica, www.iadb.org/idbamerica/index.cfm?thisid=3861.

Instituto Brasileiro de Geografia e Estatística (IBGE), 2007, www.ibge.gov.br.

Japan Bank for International Cooperation. JBIC Sector Study Series 2004. No. 2: "Sector Study for Education in Brazil." November 2005.

Korten, David. *Getting to the 21st Century: Voluntary Action and the Global Agenda.* Hartford, CT: Kumarian Press, 1990.

————. *When Corporations Rule the World.* West Hartford, CT: Kumarian Press and Berrett-Koehler Publishers, 1995.

Levine, Daniel H. "The Future of Christianity in Latin America." *Journal of Latin American Studies* vol. 41, issue 1, February 2009: 121–45.

Levine, Robert, and John J. Crocitti, eds. *The Brazil Reader: History, Culture, Politics.* Durham, NC: Duke University Press, 1999.

Lima, Elynalia. "Projeto seringueiro: 25 anos de ensino pioneiro na Floresta." October 25, 2008, http://www.ac.gov.br/bibliotecadafloresta/biblioteca.

Literacy Exchange. World Resources on Literacy, UNESCO. June 6, 2005, http://www1.uni-hamburg.de/UNESCO UIE/literacyexchange/brazil/.

Maxwell, Kenneth. *Naked Tropics: Essays on Empire and Other Rogues.* London: Routledge, 2003.

———. *The Politics of the Possible: The Brazilian Rural Workers' Union Movement, 1964–1985.* Philadelphia: Temple University Press, 1994.

Mendes, Chico. *Fight for the Forest: Chico Mendes in His Own Words.* Translated by Chris Whitehouse, additional material Tony Gross, edited by Duncan Green. London: Latin American Bureau, 1989. Adapted from Cândido Grabowski, ed. *O Testamento da Floresta.* Rio de Janeiro: FASE, 1989.

———. Personal letter to Dom Moacyr Grechi, July 29, 1987.

Millard, Candice. *The River of Doubt: Theodore Roosevelt's Darkest Journey.* New York: Broadway Books, 2005.

Mota, Aldenir Rodrigues, Alzenite de Araújo Verçosa, Cosmo Araújo e Araújo, Maria Mavy Dourado de Souza, Rosineide Rodrigues Lopes, Zairinéia Soares de Lima, and Zilah Carvalho Mastub de Oliveira. "A Formação do Partido dos Trabalhadores em Xapuri: Os 15 Anos do PT." *Xapurys* 1. Rio Branco: UFAC/DH, 1995: 21–22, 23.

Mota, Aldenir Rodrigues, Alzenite de Araújo Verçosa, Cosmo Araújo e Araújo, Rosineide Rodrigues Lopes, Zairinéia Soares de Lima, Zilah Carvalho Mastub de Oliveira. "Empate pela Vida e Defesa da Floresta em Xapuri." *Xapurys* 2. Rio Branco: UFAC/DH, 1996.

Oliveira, Edir Figueira Marques de. *Educação Básica no Acre 1962–1983, Imposição política ou pressão social?* Rio Branco: EFM, 2000.

Oliveira, Luiz Antônio Pinto de. *O Sertanejo, o Brabo e o Posseiro (Os cem anos de andanças da população acreana).* Rio Branco: Universidade Federal do Acre [UFAC], 1985.

Paulo, Amós D'Avila de, Angela Maria Gomes Alves, Caticilene Rodrigues, Rosilene da Silva, Valcidene Soares Menezes. "Soldados da Borracha de Xapuri: Memórias de um Viver." *Xapurys* 1. Rio Branco: UFAC/DH, 1995, 9, 14.

Price, David. *Before the Bulldozer: The Nambiquara Indians and the World Bank.* Cabin John, MD: Seven Locks Press, 1989.

Rabben, Linda. *Brazil's Indians and the Onslaught of Civilization: The Yanomami and the Kayapó.* Seattle: University of Washington Press, 2004.

Revkin, Andrew. *The Burning Season: The Murder of Chico Mendes and the Fight for the Amazon Rain Forest.* New York: Penguin, 1990.

Rodrigues, Gomercindo. *Walking the Forest with Chico Mendes: Struggle for Justice in the Amazon.* Translated by Linda Rabben. Austin: University of Texas Press, 2007.

Sadlier, Darlene J. *Brazil Imagined: 1500 to the Present.* Austin: University of Texas Press, 2008.

Schmink, Marianne, and Charles H. Wood. *Contested Frontiers in Amazonia.* New York: Columbia University Press, 1992.

———, eds. *Frontier Expansion in Amazonia.* Gainesville: University of Florida Press, 1984.

Schwartzman, Stephan. "Mercados para Produtos Extrativistas da Amazônia Brasileira." In Arnt, ed., *O Destino da Floresta,* 247–257.

Seminário da Poronga. Poronga Evaluation Seminar with Paulo Freire. São Paulo, August 1982. Archives of CEDOP, Curitiba. Seminar report also available online from Marina Silva Biblioteca da Floresta, http://www.ac.gov.br/ bibliotecadafloresta.

Silva, Maria do Perpétuo Socorro, José Rodrigues Arimatéia, and Frankcinato da Silva Batista. *Seringueiros, Memória, História e Identidade.* Vol. 1. Rio Branco: UFAC, Centro de Documentação e Informação Histórica, 1997.

Skidmore, Thomas E. *Brazil: Five Centuries of Change.* New York: Oxford University Press, 1999.

Slater, Candace. *Entangled Edens: Visions of the Amazon.* Berkeley: University of California Press, 2002.

Veltmeyer, Henry, and Anthony O'Malley. *Transcending Neoliberalism: Community-Based Development in Latin America.* West Hartford, CT: Kumarian Press, 2001.

Weinstein, Barbara. *The Amazon Rubber Boom, 1850–1920.* Stanford, CA: Stanford University Press, 1983.

Glossary of Portuguese Terms

Acompanhar	to supervise, train, mentor, encourage and accompany teachers
Borracha	rubber
Caboclo	rural person of mixed Indian, African, and/or European heritage
Cartilha	text
Colocação	family settlement in forest
Conscientização	the process of raising political and social consciousness
Cortar seringa	to tap rubber
Empate	nonviolent stand-off
Encontro Nacional de Seringueiros	National Encounter of Rubber Tappers
Ensino rural	rural education
Escolativa	Active school, rural education program
Farinha	ground manioc flour
Forró	type of country music originally from Northeast Brazil
Marreteiro	middleman
Mutirão	volunteer work group on community project
Patrão	(patrões, pl.) boss
Poronga	head lantern worn by rubber tappers
Pro-Formação	Pro-Formation
Seringal	(seringais, pl.) rubber estate
Seringalista	rubber estate owner
Seringueiro	rubber tapper
Sindicato	union

Acronyms

CEBs	Christian Base Communities
CEDI	Ecumenical Center for Documentation and Information
CESE	Ecumenical Coordinator of Services
CNBB	National Conference of Brazilian Bishops
CNS	National Council of Rubber Tappers
CPI	Pro-Indian Commission
CTA	Amazonian Workers Center
CUT	Workers Central Union
EMBRAPA	Brazilian Agricultural Research Corporation
FUNDEF	Fund for the Maintenance and Development of Fundamental Education
FUNTAC	Technological Foundation of Acre
INCRA	National Institute of Colonization and Agrarian Reform
MEB	Base Education Movement
MEC	Ministry of Education and Culture
PCdoB	Communist Party of Brazil
PRC	Revolutionary Communist Party
PT	Workers Party
STRX	Xapuri Rural Workers Union
UFAC	Federal University of Acre

Index

Abaloni, Paulo (padre), 139
Ação Educativa (Educational Action), 140
Acre, xi, 3–17, 131
  CEDOP-AM NGO in, 24
  illiteracy of, xii, 6
  infant mortality in, 5
  landholders/conglomerates ownership of, 8
  literacy rate of, 5
  logging in, 6
  map of, 3
  Moacyr and, 9–10, 31, 71, 88, 113–14, 129, 139
  population of, 4
  ranching destruction in, 7
Acre Women's Network, da Silva, Ivanilde, founding of, 116
adult literacy, 134
  Freire on, 25
  Projeto Seringueiro experiment of, 19
Agrarian Reform and Culture, 13
AIDS, in Brazil, 4
Alagoas seringal, Allegretti thesis on, 23
Allegretti, Mary, 12, 13–14, 19, 23, 49, 54, 64, 70, 72, 88, 129, 131, 156
  CTA creation of, 24, 92, 130
Almanaque Abril encyclopedia, 98, 102
Amazon, xi
  development policy for, 7–9
  environmental policy in, 13, 75
  images of, 3
  low income level/poverty of, 5–6

Amazonian Workers Center (CTA), 27, 40, 46, 103, 140, 143
  Allegretti creation of, 24, 92, 130
  pedagogical project of, 125
  teaching materials/teacher mentoring by, 33, 88
Amazonian Workers Center/Projeto Seringueiro (CTA/PS), 43, 56
  Itaú/UNICEF Prize for, 49
  Zaire as consultant to, 68
Amazonian Work Group. See Grupo de Trabalho Amazônico
Amnesty International, 15
Animals booklet, 101–2
animal stories, teaching materials of, 101–2
Aquino, Leide, 54
assassination, of Mendes, Chico, 10, 14, 41, 43, 85, 91, 92, 128, 133, 150
Association of Sick Persons, da Silva, Ivanilde, founding of, 116
Association of Working Men and Women, da Silva, Ivanilde, founding of, 116

Baldassari, Paolino (padre), church-school of, 21
Barbosa, Júlio, 11, 74, 137, 139
de Barros, Raimundo, 11, 20, 24, 43, 137, 139, 156
base community. See Christian base communities
Base Education Movement. See Movimento de Educação de Base

basic education, 124–25
  in Brazil, 5–7, 25
  Fundef push for, 36
Benjamin, Walter, 140
Boa Vista seringal, 71
  school in, 33
Boff, Clodovis, 145
Boff, Leonardo, 30, 71, 145
Bom Destino seringal, 106
Brazil, 5, 12, 14, 30
  AIDS in, 4
  democracy of, 3–32
  education context of, 5–7
  ethanol fuel exporter, 55
  Freire influence on education of, 25
  government incentives of, 7
  map of, 2
  military government of, 7
Brazilian Agricultural Research Enterprise.
    See Empresa Brasileira de Pesquisa
    Agropecuária

Cachoeira reserve, 13
  empate of, 35
  school in, 59, 90
Cámara, Helder, 145
Campbell, Constance, 35
capitalism
  liberation theology rejection of, 29
  Moacyr on, 31
de Castelo, Reginaldo, 41, 92, 140
Catholic Church, 28, 142
  financial support of, 88
  radio program of, 9
  as rubber tapper sanctuary, 9, 152
Catuaba empate, 115
CDT. See Commission in Defense of
    the Worker
CEBs. See Christian base communities
CEDI. See Centro Ecumênico de
    Documentação e Informação
CEDOP-AM NGO, in Acre, Allegretti
    creation of, 24
Central Única de Trabalhadores (CUT)
    (Workers Central Union), 15
  Chico Mendes school of, 115–16
Centro Ecumênico de Documentação e
    Informação (CEDI) (Ecumenical
    Center for Documentation and
    Information), 25, 27, 72, 140, 153

CESE. See Coordinadora Ecuménica
    de Serviços
de Chardin, Teilhard, 145
Chico Mendes Extractive Reserve, 14
Chico Mendes school of CUT, 115–16
Christian base communities (CEBs), 72,
    113, 150
  in Latin America, 30
  liberation theology of, xiii, 9, 35, 114
  Projeto Seringueiro influence by, 78
  school creation in, 35, 75
  school/medical services request by, 21
  seringueiros mobilization and, 35
  da Silva, Ivanilde, and, 127–28
  union organization and, 10
Christianity and Social Progress.
    See Mater et Magistra
church-schools, in Sena Madureira, 21
civil-society, of NGOs, 110, 143
Clodovis (padre), 71
Clóvis, Gumercindo, 139
CNBB. See National Bishops' Council
CNS. See National Rubber Tappers'
    Council
Comblin, José, 145
Comissâo Pro Indio (CPI) (Pro-Indian
    Commission), 50, 135, 142
  financial support of, 88
  on Poronga text, 53
Commission in Defense of the Worker
    (CDT), 129
Communist Party of Brazil (PCdoB), 31,
    127, 132, 139
condom factory, in Xapuri, 4
conscientization, 75, 117
  Freire educational method of, 30, 104
conservation, Projeto Seringueiro
    emphasis on, 35
CONTAG (rural labor federation), 12
cooperative, 30, 56, 90, 129
  initial, failure of, 35
  reading necessity for, 72
  school connection with, 22
  school separation from, 33
  of seringueiros, 14–15
  success of, 95
Coordinadora Ecuménica de Serviços
    (CESE), 88, 94
country comparison game teaching
    material, 102–3

CPI. *See* Comissâo Pro Indio
CPT. *See* Pastoral Land Commissions
CTA. *See* Amazonian Workers Center
CTA/PS. *See* Amazonian Workers
    Center/Projeto Seringueiro
culture, preservation of, xi, 96, 136
culture of silence, Freire on, 25
da Cunha, Manoel Estébio Cavalcante,
    19, 24, 43, 45, 46, 50, 54, 56, 72,
    96, 97, 110, 124, 125, 128–45,
    151, 152, 156
    as Indigenous Education office
      director, 50
    PCdoB and, 31
    teacher training course of, 40
CUT. *See* Central Única de
    Trabalhadores

Dantas, Andréa Maria Lopes, 105
Dantas, Wanderley, 7
deforestation, 12, 32, 55, 76, 83–84,
    115, 137, 141
democracy, of Brazil, 3–32
Department of Indigenous Education,
    53
Department of Rural Education, 53
Derickx, João, 132
Deustro, Cláudio (padre), 71, 129, 139
Deustro, Otávio (padre), 71
developmentalism, social justice and, 29
developmentalist capitalism, Gutiérrez
    on, 29
development policy, of Amazon, 7–9
disarray, of Projeto Seringueiro, 39–41,
    89, 150
dislocation, of seringueiros, 8, 19, 144

economic exploitation, xii, 30
school objective to end, 64–65
economic freedom, as objective of
    Projeto Seringueiro, 19, 150, 153
economic globalization, xiii, 36, 130
Ecumenical Center for Documentation
    and Information. *See* Centro
    Ecumênico de Documentação
    e Informação
*Educação Matemática na Floresta (Math
    Education in the Forest)*, 100
Educação para Todos (Education for All),
    49–52

education, xi. *See also* literacy
    basic, 5–7, 36, 124–25
    culture/habitat as basis of, 149, 155
    elementary, 5
    health, 73
    indigenous, 43, 136, 143
    liberating, xiv, 26
    NGOs and, 50–51, 143
    popular, xii, 25, 48, 72, 130, 149, 153
    rural, 49, 68–69, 109–45, 117
    university, for teachers of Projeto
      Seringueiro, 51–52, 137, 144
Educational Action, 140
educational revolution, xii
    empowerment for, 149, 155
Education for All. *See* Educação
    para Todos
elementary education, universal access
    to, 5
EMBRAPA. *See* Empresa Brasileira de
    Pesquisa Agropecuária
empate (nonviolent standoff), 13,
    82, 152
    of Cachoeira, 35
    in Catuaba, 115
    locations of, 12
    Mendes, Chico, on, 11–12
    Pinheiro and, 11
    at Santa Fé seringal, 20, 131–32
empowerment, xi, 37, 153
    of education based on culture/habitat,
      149, 155
    Poronga text on, 23–24
    by Projeto Seringueiro, 35
    of seringueiros, 10, 27–28
Empresa Brasileira de Pesquisa
    Agropecuária (EMBRAPA)
    (Brazilian Agricultural Research
    Enterprise), 15, 32, 134
Encontro Nacional de Seringueiros
    da Amazônia (National Encounter
    of Amazonian Rubber Tappers),
    12–13, 14, 37, 39, 130–31, 153
Environmental Defense Fund, 32
environmentalism, xiii, 28, 127
    of North Americans, 13
    Projeto Seringueiro influence by,
      32–33, 154
environmental policy, in Amazon, 13, 75
environmental protection, 76, 81, 83–84

Equador, 12
  empate of estate of, 13
Escolativa rural education program, 49,
    68–69, 135–36, 144
Estébio, Manoel, 73–74
exploitation, of seringueiros, 20, 24
extractive reserves, 12, 30, 32, 37, 39,
    44–49, 56, 105, 133, 138
  decree of, 41
  development/environmental
    protection, 13–14
  Mendes, Chico, on, 13

Federal University of Acre.
  See Universidade Federal do Acre
Federal University of Rio de Janeiro.
  See Universidade Federal do Rio
  de Janeiro
Feitosa, Júlia, 86, 92
Ferreira, Djalcir "Pingo," 50, 54, 56, 68,
    85–86, 95–108, 123, 124, 151,
    156–57
  teacher training/curriculum
    development by, 44, 45–46, 48–49,
    51, 93, 133–34
Filho, Armando Soares, 72, 87, 130
financial support
  of Catholic Church, 88
  of CPI, 88
  of FUNARTE, 88
  funding reports for, 94–95
  of MEC, 24, 88, 130
  of Oxfam, 24, 88, 129, 130, 131
da Floresta, Marina Silva Biblioteca, 54
Floresta seringal, 20
  school in, 33
forest habitat, xi
  clearing/burning of, 7, 74
  defense of, 9–15
  management of, 76
Forest Path. See O Varadouro newspaper
forest people, xiii
  CTA/PS education for, 49
  tradition/customs of, 66
Fragoso, António, 145
Freire, Paulo, 19, 36, 86, 107–8,
    133, 140
  conscientization education method of,
    30, 104
  pedagogical principles of, 122–23, 150

popular education advocated by, xiii,
    25, 48, 72, 130
Poronga text influence by, 23–24
Projeto Seringueiro influence of,
    25–28, 33–34, 108, 151
FUNAI government Indian protection
    agency, 141
FUNARTE, financial support of, 88
Fundação Roberto Marino, 143
Fundção Tecnológica do Acre
    (FUNTAC) (Technological
    Foundation of Acre), 46, 105
Fundef. *See* Fund for the Development
    of Fundamental Education and
    Enhancement of the Teachers'
    Profession
Fund for the Development of
    Fundamental Education and
    Enhancement of the Teachers'
    Profession (Fundef), 5
  basic education push by, 36
  funding reports, for financial support,
    94–95
FUNTAC. *See* Fundção Tecnológica
    do Acre

Geisel, Ernesto, 36
gender equality, of Projeto Seringueiro,
    52–53, 70, 96–97, 138
global factors, of rancher/logger, 8
Gore, Al, 76
government
  incentives, 7
  Mendes, Chico, distrust of, 89
  teacher salary paid by, 88
Gross, Tony, 12, 19
Grupo de Pesquisa e Extensão em
    Sisternas Agroflorestais do Acre
    (PESACRE) (Research Extension
    Group in Agriforestry Systems of
    Acre), 15
Grupo de Trabalho Amazônico (GTA)
    (Amazonian Work Group), 15
GTA. *See* Grupo de Trabalho Amazônico
Guevara, Ernesto "Che," 31, 107, 115,
    141, 152
Gutiérrez, Gustavo, 28, 29, 145

Haddad, Sérgio, 140
Hara, Regina, 141

health education, 73
Higino, Ivair, 13

illiteracy
    of Acre, xii, 6
    of Mendes, Chico, 22–23
immigration, uncontrolled, 7
income, Amazon low level of, 5–6
An Inconvenient Truth (Gore), 76
INCRA land reform agency, 115, 130
indigenism, 142
indigenous education, 53
    rescue/rehabilitation of, 136
    state function of, 143
Indigenous Education office, of Acre, da
    Cunha as director of, 50
indigenous population, 136, 151
individualism, 71, 76
Industry and Commerce, Education,
    Health, Agriculture, ministries
    of, 13
infant mortality, of Acre, 5
institutionalization, 110, 150, 154
intellectual ferment (1970/1980s), xiii
intellectual universe of knowledge, 46
    Freire on, 25–26
interfamilial relationships, school
    teaching of, 70
international lending institutions, 13
Itaú/UNICEF Prize, of CTA/PS, 49

John Paul II (pope), 29–30
John XXIII (pope), 28
Joia, Rando, 140
Justiça e Paz (Justice and Peace)
    movement, 145
justice, struggle for liberation theology
    and, 28
Justice and Peace. *See Justiça e Paz*
    movement

Kaxinawá, 136
Klein, Paulo, 72, 129
Kuntz, Alfred, 145

labor force, land speculator expulsion
    of, 8
Landless Movement. *See Sem Terra*
land speculators, xiii, 7–8
    labor force expulsion by, 8, 13

Latin America
    CEBs/conscientization of, 30
    Freire influence on education of, 25
    liberation theology development and,
        28–30
The Lesson of the Samaúma Tree, 45
liberating education, xiv, 26
liberation theology, xiii, 9, 56, 139,
    142, 152
    capitalism/socialism rejection by, 29
    CEBs and, xiii, 9, 35, 114
    of da Cunha, 144–45
    Marxism and, 29
    poverty and, 28
    Projeto Seringueiro influence by,
        27–30, 151–52
    social movement and, 21
    struggle for justice and, 28
    Teles, Dercy, and, 71
    Vatican II and, 29
Liberation Theology (Gutiérrez), 145
A Lição da Samaúma (The Lesson of the
    Samaúma Tree), 45, 104
literacy, xi, 72, 77, 123, 134, 150.
    See also illiteracy
    Friere on, 26
    rates, for Acre, 5
    of Rio Branco, 5
loggers, xiii
    global factors for, 8
logging, in Acre, xi, 6
Luxembourg, Rosa, 140

Mala de Leitura (Suitcase of Readings),
    66–67, 134
malaria, 5
Maracajú seringal, 110
Marques, Arnóbio "Binho," 40, 44, 54,
    56, 69, 82, 85, 89, 96, 97, 105,
    117, 123–24, 127, 132, 134–35,
    139, 143, 152, 156
    CNS disagreement by, 43
    PCdoB and, 31
    Projeto Seringueiro stabilization by,
        42–43
    as SEC/AC, 49–50
    teacher university education and,
        51–52
Martins, Maria Lúcia, 108
Marxism, xiii, 21, 92, 96, 139–40

liberation theology and, 29
Projeto Seringueiro influence by, 28, 30–32, 152
Masagáo, Vera, 140
Mater et Magistra (Christianity and Social Progress), 28
math, seringueiro need for, 24
Math Education in the Forest. See Educação Matemática na Floresta
MEB. *See* Movimento de Educação de Base
MEC. *See* Ministry of Education and Culture, Brazilian
Medellin conference, 29, 139
medical services
    CEBs request for, 21
    Klein and, 72
    for preventative health, 74
Mendes, Chico, xiii, 11–12, 13, 19, 24, 27, 30, 32, 37, 54, 56, 64, 70, 80, 86, 127, 131, 139, 142, 153, 155–56
    assassination of, 10, 14, 41, 43, 85, 91, 92, 128, 133, 150
    government distrust by, 89
    illiteracy of, 22–23
    PCdoB and, 31
    persuasion of, 22
    Projeto Seringueiro revival of, 42
    PT membership of, 87
    STR support by, 40
Mendes, Duda, 79
Mendes, Nilson, 81
de Menezes, Luiz Carlos, 107, 108
Mestre, Carlos, 71
methodology, of conditions in seringal, 24–25
middlemen, seringueiros exploitation by, 20
Migaña, José (padre), 114
migration, 7, 96, 138
Militão, Jair, 107
Ministry of Education and Culture (MEC), Brazilian
    financial support of, 24, 88, 130
    school project with, 90
    social movement and, 101
    teaching materials of, 47, 97–100, 106
Moacyr, Grechi (Dom), 9–10, 31, 71, 88, 113–14, 129, 139

mobilization, of seringueiros, xiii, 35, 131–32, 150, 153
Mohan, Edgar, 108
monopoly, of patróes, 19
Morini, Alberto (padre), 127
Mourão, Nilson, 71, 114
Movimento de Educação de Base (MEB) (Base Education Movement), 74, 133
mutirão (volunteer work groups), 69

National Bishops' Council (CNBB), 88
National Encounter of Amazonian Rubber Tappers. *See* Encontro Nacional de Seringueiros da Amazônia
National Rubber Tappers' Council (CNS), 14, 27, 43, 56, 131, 133
    Marques disagreement with, 43, 91
Nazaré seringal, 12, 19, 49, 88, 129
    mobilization of, 24
    original school in, 33, 153
    strengthening of, 20
NGOs, xi, 125, 131, 156, 157
    CEDI, 25, 27, 72, 140, 153
    CEDOP-AM, 24
    CESE, 88, 129
    civil-society of, 110, 143
    CPI, 50, 53, 88, 135, 142
    educational in São Paulo, 25
    education and, 50–51, 143
    Fundação Roberto Marino, 143
    national/international, Projeto Seringueiro alliances with, 32
    Oxfam, 15, 24, 88, 129
    PESACRE, 15
    Projeto Seringueiro involvement by, 34, 55
    role of, 85, 94, 135
    union cooperation with, 32
nonviolent standoff. *See* empate
North Americans, environmentalism of, 13
Northeast region, school attendance in, 6

Office of Rural Education, 117, 126
de Oliveira, Marlete, 24, 72, 87, 131
de Oliveira, Ronaldo, 24, 72, 87, 129, 130–31, 140, 141–42
de Oliveira, Socorro D'Avila, 66, 98, 103

oppression
Freire struggle against, 25
of labor by capital, 31
oral culture, of seringueiros, 21, 37, 67,
104, 111, 122
O Varadouro (*Forest Path*) newspaper, 36
Oxfam, 15, 131
financial support of, 24, 88, 129,
130, 131

Pacem in Terris (Peace on Earth), 28
Partido dos Trabalhadores (PT) (Workers
Party), 12, 30, 33, 40, 56, 103,
127, 139, 142
Mendes, Chico, as member of, 87
PCdoB and, 31
Partido Revolucionario Comunista
(PRC)(Revolutionary Communist
Party), 87
Pastoral Land Commissions (CPT),
10, 152
patróes (rubber estate owners),
monopoly of, 19
PCdoB. *See* Communist Party of Brazil
Peace on Earth. *See Pacem in Terris*
pedagogical principles, of Freire,
122–23, 150
pedagogical project, of CTA, 125
Pedagogy of the Oppressed (Freire), 140
Pereira, Ademir Rodriguez, 46, 54, 63,
64–71, 103, 156
Pereira, Antonia, 63–64, 78–84,
149, 154
PESACRE. *See* Grupo de Pesquisa e
Extensão em Sisternas Agroflorestais
do Acre
Pinheiro, Wilson, 11
murder of, 12
Political-Pedagogical Project. *See Projeto
Politico Pedagógico*
political revolution, xii
Projeto Seringueiro for, 90
political skill development, of
seringuerios, 19, 27
Pontifical Catholic University (PUC),
104, 107
popular education
Freire advocacy of, xiii, 25, 48, 72, 130
program, 149, 153
population, of Acre, 4

Poronga text, 25, 53, 79, 104, 123, 129
CEDI evaluation of, 27, 140
empowerment focus of, 23–24
poverty, 111
in Amazon, 5–6
CEBs/conscientization and, 30
Freire struggle against, 25
liberation theology and, 28
paternalism and, 25
PRC. *See* Revolutionary Communist
Party
Proambiente, on rural health/
environment, 75
Pro-Formação, 137
Pro-formation (Pro-formação)
program, 77
teaching standardization by, 51
Pro-Indian Commission. *See* Comissáo
Pro Indio
Project Rubber Tapper. *See* Projeto
Seringueiro
Projeto Politico Pedagógico (Political-
Pedagogical Project), 105–6
Projeto Seringueiro (Project Rubber
Tapper), 6–7
adult literacy experiment of, 19
affirmations of, 34
CEBs influence on, 78
CEDI revision of materials of, 27, 140
conservation emphasis of, 35
cooperative direction by, 90
culture preservation and, xi, 96, 136
disarray of, 39–41, 89, 150
early years of, 33–37
economic freedom objective of, 19,
150, 153
environmentalism influence on,
32–33
expanding influence of, 41
Freire influence on, 25–28, 33–34,
108, 151
gender equality of, 52–53, 70,
96–97, 138
history of, 150–52
influence/legacy of, 52–56
influences on, 25–33
lessons of, 155
liberation theology influence on,
27–30, 151–52
Marxism influence on, 28, 30–32, 152

national/international NGOs alliances of, 32

NGOs involvement with, 34, 55

origins of, 19–25

partisan control independence of, 33–34

problem-solving skills of, 153

public policy of, 125, 135, 156

renewal of, 42–44, 150

rural education influence by, 117–18

to rural/indigenous education, 109–45

success reasons, 153–54

teachers of, 24, 33, 39, 46, 51–52, 63, 64–71, 78–84, 88, 95–96, 103, 136–37

PT. *See* Partido dos Trabalhadores

public policy, of Projeto Seringueiro, 125, 135, 149, 156

PUC. *See* Pontifical Catholic University

Puebla conference, 29

radio program, of Catholic Church, 9

rainforest. *See* tropical rainforest

Rainforest Alliance, 32

ranchers, xiii

global factors for, 8

Projeto Seringueiro confrontation of, 90

repression from, 12

Santa Fé burning by, 20

ranching interests, xi

Acre damage by, 7

reformers

Ferreira, 85–86, 95–108

Marques, 85, 87–95

religion, xi. *See also* Catholic Church; Christian base communities

of da Silva, Ivanilde, 13–114

Research Extension Group in Agriforestry Systems of Acre. *See* Grupo de Pesquisa e Extensão em Sisternas Agroflorestais do Acre

Revolutionary Communist Party. *See* Partido Revolucionario Comunista

Ribeirinho (Riverbank Dweller), 133

Rio Branco, 36, 66, 74, 115, 119, 128, 139, 140, 142

immigrants from rubber estates in, 8

literacy rates of, 5

public works/beautification campaigns of, 4

teaching workshops at, 46

Riverbank Dweller. *See Ribeirinho*

rubber estate owners. *See* patróes

rubber tappers. *See* seringueiros

rural education, 109–45

Escolativa program of, 49, 68–69, 135–36, 144

Projeto Seringueiro influence on, 117–18

da Silva, Ivanilde, as team member for, 117

rural labor federation. *See* CONTAG

rural movement, of Xapuri, 71

Santa Fé seringal

empate at, 20, 131–32

ranchers burning of, 20

school in, 33

São Francisco school, 59

São Paulo, 104

educational NGO in, 25

São Pedro seringal, 129, 131

school in, 33

Schemberg, Mário, 108

school

CEBs creation of, 35, 75

CEBs request for, 21

cooperative connection with, 22

economic exploitation, objective to end, 64–65

interfamilial/social relationships teaching in, 70

MEC project with, 90

Northeast region attendance in, 6

Political-Pedagogical Project requirement in, 105–6

in seringals, 33, 59, 90

seringueiros establishment of, 20

state commitment to provide resources for, 4

as sustaining force, in community, 35

SEC/AC. *See* secretary of education for Acre

Second Vatican Council, 28

secretary of education for Acre (SEC/AC), 46, 68

Marques as, 49–50, 85, 91

Secretary of Education Rural Education, 86
Sem Terra (Landless Movement), 140
Sena Madureira, 5, 14
  church-schools in, 21
seringal
  Alagoas, 23
  Boa Vista, 33, 71
  Bom Desino, 106
  Floresta, 20, 33
  Maracajú, 110
  methodology adapted to, 24–25
  Nazaré, 12, 19, 20, 24, 33, 49, 88, 129
  retention in, 67
  Santa Fé, 20, 33, 131–32
  Tupac, 129
seringueiros (rubber tappers), xi
  de Castelo on arming of, 92
  Catholic church as sanctuary for, 9, 152
  cooperative of, 14–15
  dislocation of, 8, 19, 144
  empowerment of, 10, 27–28
  math need of, 24
  middlemen exploitation of, 20
  mistrust by, 20
  mobilization of, xiii, 35, 131–32, 150, 153
  oral culture of, 21, 37, 67, 104, 111, 122
  organization by, 9
  political skill development of, 19
  school establishment by, 20
  testimony of, xiv, 64–145
  union of, xiii, 10, 23, 32, 72, 75, 80
  U.S. environmentalist alliance with, 13
Silva, Marina, 11, 43, 89
da Silva, Cila Pereira, 66, 134
da Silva, Francisca "Chiquinha," 44, 53, 56, 96, 105, 109–10, 118–28, 135, 154, 156–57
da Silva, Ivanilde Lopes, 53, 109–18, 152
  CEBs and, 127–28
de Silva, Inácio "Lula," 43
Sindicato de Trabalhadores Rurais (STR) (Union of Rural Workers), xiv, 27, 43, 56, 152
  da Cunha and, 128–29

Mendes, Chico, support of, 40
Teles, Dercy, as president of, 129
socialism, liberation theology rejection of, 29
social justice
  developmentalism and, 29
  UFAC for, 36
social movement, xi, 21, 54, 114, 125, 129, 142, 151
  MEC ignorance of, 101
social relationships, school teaching of, 70
STR. *See* Sindicato de Trabalhadores Rurais
strategic plan, for school, 105–6, 126
STRX. *See* Xapuri Rural Workers' Union
sugar cane plantations, 76, 154
Suitcase of Readings. *See Mala de Leitura*

Távora, Euclides Fernandes, 10
teachers, of Projeto Seringueiro, 24
  criteria/requirements for, 46, 67
  CTA mentoring of, 33, 88
  government salary for, 88
  Pereira, Ademir, 63, 64–71
  Pereira, Antonia, 78–84
  rehabilitation project for, 136–37
  salary, lack of, 39
  training course evaluation of, 103
  university education for, 51–52, 137, 144
  unschooled, lay, 95–96, 136–37
Teachers Union, in Rio Branco, da Silva, Ivanilde, direction of, 116
teacher training course, 46–47, 83, 98–99, 124, 130, 132, 154
  of CTA/PS, 46
  of da Cunha, 40
  of Ferreira, 44, 45–46, 48–49, 51, 93, 133–34
  Marques and, 89
  Pereira, Ademir, on, 67
  teacher evaluation in, 103
teaching materials
  Almanaque Abril encyclopedia, 98, 102
  Animal booklet, 101–2
  of animal stories, 101–2
  of country comparison game, 102–3
  CTA production of, 33, 88
  da Cunha development of, 45

Educação Matemática na Floresta, 100
on environment, 154
Ferreira development of, 44
A Lição da Samaúra text, 45, 104
Mala de Leitura, 66–67, 98, 134
of MEC, 47, 97–100, 106
Pacem in Terris, 28
Poronga text, 23–24, 25, 27, 53, 79,
    104, 123, 129, 140
Pro-formation standardization of, 51
relevance of, 155
Ribeirinho, 133
Technological Foundation of Acre. *See*
    Fundção Tecnológica do Acre
Teles, Dercy, 24, 41, 63, 71–78, 79, 129,
    130, 152, 154
Teles, Pedro, 64
testimony, of seringueiros, xiv
    of da Cunha, 128–45
    of Marques, 87–95
    of Pereira, Ademir, 64–70
    of Pereira, Antonia, 78–84
    of reformers, 85–108
    of da Silva, Francisca, 118–28
    of da Silva, Ivanilde, 110–18
    of Teles, Dercy, 71–78
theology. *See* liberation theology
Todos Somos Irmãos (We Are All Brothers
    and Sisters) radio program, 9
Torres, Camilo, 145
traditions/customs, of forest people, 66
tropical rainforest, 4
    clearing/burning of, 7
    defense of, 154
    deforestation of, 12, 32, 55, 76,
        83–84, 115, 137, 141
Tupac seringal, 129
Turrini, Heitor (padre), 128

UFAC. *See* Universidade Federal do Acre
UFRJ. *See* Universidade Federal do Rio
    de Janeiro
UNESCO, Freire work with, 25
UNICAMP, 141
UNICEF, xii, 49, 143
union, of seringueiros, xiii, 10, 72,
    80, 150
    as defense, 23
    finances of, 75

NGOs cooperation with, 32
Union of Rural Workers. *See* Sindicato
    de Trabalhadores Rurais
Universidade Federal do Acre (UFAC)
    (Federal University of Acre), 36, 85,
    105, 122–23, 139, 140
Universidade Federal do Rio de Janeiro
    (UFRJ) (Federal University of Rio
    de Janeiro), 85
university education, for teachers
    of Projeto Seringueiro, 51–52,
    137, 144
University of Campinas, 123
University of São Paulo (USP),
    104, 107
USP. *See* University of São Paulo

Vatican II, liberation theology and, 29
Vaz, Fábio, 89, 92
Viana, Jorge, 4, 44, 49, 56, 69, 75, 82,
    91–92, 105, 115, 117, 123, 125,
    127, 134–35, 143, 151
Virillo, Paul, 108
volunteer work groups. *See mutirão*

We Are All Brothers and Sisters.
    See Todos Somos Irmãos
Winter, Eloisa, 72, 140
Workers Central Union. *See* Central
    Única de Trabalhadores
Workers Party. *See* Partido dos
    Trabalhadores
World Council of Churches, 88
World Wildlife Federation, 15

Xapuri, xi, 5, 11, 14, 67, 125, 140
    condom factory in, 4
    cooperative, 35
    Projeto Seringueiro commemoration
        in, 54, 151–52
    Projeto Seringueiro's early history and,
        34–35
    rural movement of, 71
    syndicates in, 21
    teaching workshops at, 46
Xapuri Rural Workers' Union (STRX),
    10, 30, 63

Zaire, Graciete, 68, 105

About the Author

enis Heyck is Professor of Spanish at Loyola University Chicago, where she teaches Latin American Culture and Literature, and where she received the Edwin T. and Vivijeanne F. Sujack Award for Teaching Excellence. Professor Heyck has published a book of oral histories, *Life Stories of the Nicaraguan Revolution* (Routledge, 1990); an anthology on Latino cultures in the United States, *Barrios and Borderlands* (Routledge, 1994); a book of interviews dealing with the impact of globalization and development on local cultures in Latin America, *Surviving Globalization* (Broadview Press, 2002); and a book of readings on tradition and change in key aspects of Latin American culture, *Tradición y cambio* (McGraw-Hill, 3rd ed., 2005). She received her PhD from the University of London.

Also from Kumarian Press...

Latin American Studies:

Mobilizing for Human Rights in Latin America
Edward Cleary

Inside El Barrio:
A Bottom-Up View of Neighborhood Life in Castro's Cuba
Henry Louis Taylor Jr.

Trapped:
Modern-Day Slavery in the Brazilian Amazon
Binka Le Breton

Confronting Globalization:
Economic Integration and Popular Resistance in Mexico
Edited by Timothy A. Wise, Hilda Salazar and Laura Carlsen

New and Forthcoming:

Rethinking Corporate Social Engagement:
Lessons from Latin America
Lester M. Salamon

From Political Won't to Political Will:
Building Support for Participatory Governance
Edited by Carmen Malena

Dispossessed People:
Establishing Legitimacy and Rights for Global Migrants
Mary Littrell and Marsha Dickson

The Change Imperative
Creating the Next Generation NGO

Visit Kumarian Press at **www.kpbooks.com** or call **toll-free**
800.232.0223 for a complete catalog.

green press
INITIATIVE

Kumarian Press, located in Sterling, Virginia, is a forward-looking, scholarly press that promotes active international engagement and an awareness of global connectedness.